THE **BEST** OF THESE IS *Love*

ANDREW NELSON

authorHOUSE®

AuthorHouse™
1663 Liberty Drive
Bloomington, IN 47403
www.authorhouse.com
Phone: 1 (800) 839-8640

This is a work of fiction. All of the characters, names, incidents, organizations, and dialogue in this novel are either the products of the author's imagination or are used fictitiously.

Published by AuthorHouse   10/27/2015

ISBN: 978-1-5049-5602-4 (sc)
ISBN: 978-1-5049-5601-7 (e)

Print information available on the last page.

Any people depicted in stock imagery provided by Thinkstock are models, and such images are being used for illustrative purposes only. Certain stock imagery © Thinkstock.

This book is printed on acid-free paper.

KJV
Scripture quotations marked KJV are from the Holy Bible, King James Version (Authorized Version). First published in 1611. Quoted from the KJV Classic Reference Bible, Copyright © 1983 by The Zondervan Corporation.

CONTENTS

Acknowledgements

My wife Janet and I were married for a bit more than fifty five years before God called her home. She was more responsible than anyone else in helping me to gain at least some understanding of what love was all about for to me her kindness and gentleness and also her wisdom gave a daily picture of God's love. But it was only after she was gone that I began to better grasp what Jesus meant when he told us to love others the way he loved us. My son Greg has also been a great help to me as he has very patiently listened to my often fuddled explanations and even offered astute comments. I also have been greatly boosted in my fiction forming by the patient ministrations of Pastors such as Captain Jay Davis of the Salvation Army where I am a soldier. I also must praise and thank Nancy and Bob Platt who have had kind comments. Nancy particularly has been like a cheer leader prodding me on when I dragged my feet too much. And I also cannot speak too highly of a recent friend of myself and my son, Susan Van Bragt, who is a great encourager. And I must add that there are many more who are encouragers, more folks that I could never begin to list. All I can say to the many who have boosted me on my way are that I love all of you and hope for God's richest blessings on every one of you.

CHAPTER ONE

A medium-build tall man paused to read a sign on the gate in the picket fence which surrounded the yards of the large two-storied residence. The sign declared the place to be Granny's Lodging. Without setting down his heavy suit case and bulky brief case he nudged the gate open. The gate's spring closed it behind him as he walked up the short sidewalk to the front porch. As he went up the steps to the front door he could dimly see his reflection on the door's pane of glass.

His image showed what a wind-blown mess his hair was after his half mile walk from the depot. It was about nine and he had been on the slow local train for almost twelve hours. It even stopped for frequent hikers along the track who flagged it down. His shoes were lightly mud spotted from crossing the puddles at the depot and his slacks and jacket were wrinkled and dusty.

He set down his luggage and leaned closer to the glass to better see to quickly comb his hair and then wipe the locomotive soot off his face with his bandana. The bits of mud on his shoes were quite dry now and he rubbed them against his cuffs to be a little more presentable. Only then did he ring the doorbell. He was not a vain person but his relatives had always told him to be careful about first impressions because you only had one chance to make them.

It was mid-September and the days were warm so that most homes had their screens up yet and many windows open. The cheery voice of a young woman called out the front kitchen window, "C'mon in. The door's not locked. I'll be with you in a jiffy after I tend to stuff in the oven. Make yourself at home and the blue door with a faucet fastened to it is what made sense to people who knew my grandpa who called rest rooms water closets. I still need to frost the cinnamon buns while they're hot so that'll give you time for whatever freshening up you wish to do."

He left his luggage on the floor outside the rest room. The small room looked and smelled clean as did the towels and face clothes. The medicine cabinet's mirror had substantial electric lights at both sides and he inspected his eyes for any appearance of being bloodshot because of his extreme lack of sleep in the past few days. He felt his bristly chin and pulled his small shaving kit out of one of his voluminous jacket pockets. His Gillette safety razor and cream out of a tube allowed him a refreshing shave. He also dampened and combed his hair.

He left his burdens along the bathroom wall where it seemed to him they would not be in the way and he sat down on a very comfortable easy chair which could have quickly lured him to sleep if he had a long wait. He had not had any breakfast and the rush of catching his train the night before had left him with no time for a meal. Thus the yeasty cinnamon roll scent awakened his hunger. And before he had hardly got comfortably settled, the young woman was rushing into the waiting room.

She wore a bit too big house dress which was very faded. It had short sleeves and the hem was midway between her knees and ankles. He heard later that it had been her grandmother's house dress for doing chores. The woman was removing a red triangular kerchief which had been effectively keeping her light brown hair in order when she previously had hung up laundry to dry that windy day. She stuffed it into the big pocket of her apron as she crossed the room to greet the newcomer. She held out her hand to him and he hastily rose to his feet, musing that he had always been taught a gentleman must let the lady be first in such matters as handshakes. Her grip was firm and not a bit like holding a dead fish which many affected.

"Are you Mr. Stone? Granny said she expected you today."

He replied, "You're right. Are you Miss Brown, her granddaughter?"

She answered," Yes, I am." She paused and looked down momentarily as if caught by surprise. "Everybody who knows me calls me Gloria. I am actually Mrs. Frank Miller."

And at this Mr. Stone was surprised for earlier that week in a phone conversation when he had made a reservation for a room for through the end of October; the older woman had mentioned that her granddaughter had a daughter over three years old. The young woman who had just welcomed him seemed much too young to have a child of that age. In the back of his mind had arisen the possibility of a pleasant association with what he thought could be a time of casual friendship. But he would never consider a relationship, even a very informal one, with a married woman.

"A few days ago Granny showed me the money order you sent her to pay for the whole time you expected to be here. And both of your trunks came two days ago and they are safely locked in your room. And she is right now coming to the gate with my little brother Mark and my daughter Maggie. You came right past the vegetable market they were getting some things from."

The spry elderly woman hustled into the house like a sudden gust of wind and shooed two children, a little girl and a bigger boy in ahead of her. Each of the trio carried grocery bags which seemed appropriate for the size of their bearers. She handed over her bag to the young lady and said, "Gloria, help the kids put away the veggies while I get acquainted with this tall handsome stranger. And are the rolls ready? And is there a fresh pot of coffee?"

Then turning to face the man she said as she held out her hand to him, "You must surely be Mr. Garth Stone. Am I correct?" She gave him a tight rapid shake that gave him a swift appraisal of her considerable strength and vigor. But her color was a bit too red and she seemed to be short-winded.

"Yes ma'am. And you must indeed be Mrs. Granny Brown."

"You're right. And we baked cinnamon rolls so you could visit with us and we could get acquainted right off the beginning. You will have a roll with us and perhaps you'd like coffee?"

"It sounds great but I do need to call Sheriff Strait. My boss, Major Colfax, has arranged for me to do business for him with the police department, the game wardens, and the public school. Do you know the Sheriff?"

Granny grinned and asked, "Was Garrison Stone your daddy?"

"Yes, ma'am."

"Son, I knew all three of them back when. So you're back in the old stomping grounds for a while? Will you need privacy for your call to Caleb?"

"No ma'am, just need to set up a meeting time with him."

"You can use our office phone right in there and shut the door for privacy."

"No privacy needed, but thank you." He dialed the number and Granny heard him say, "Uncle Caleb….. So Good to hear your voice….. Give my regards to Aunt Ellen….. She wants me over for lunch?.... Absolutely!!.... You'll pick me up at twelve thirty?.... See you then. Bye-bye."

No sooner had he hung up the phone then Gloria came out of the kitchen to invite the man in for what would be the first intake of food since he had boarded the train and his stomach was almost growling at his anticipation of what had smelled so much like the rolls his clan delighted in. And these were king-size just like from his childhood. He pondered over how simple friendly greetings and such a tasty treat could almost instantly make him feel at home. At first it was quite silent at the table as both children and the ladies began enjoying their treats with the man.

Granny was first to break the pleasant silence by asking "Were your father and the Sheriff actually relatives? I wasn't intending to overhear but you spoke quite loud and called my friend Caleb your uncle. And please pardon my nosiness."

"It's a natural question. The whole Stone clan all agree that respect should always be shown to elders. And aunt and uncle were the proper way to address older folks that were friends of the family. I've always been told to say Mr. or Mrs. or Miss to people senior to me or say ma'am or sir. We even say aunt or uncle to senior cousins. In fact in some countries any older man or woman will be addressed as Grandfather or Grandmother whether relatives or not. And I think Granny is a very respectful term even if the name on her birth certificate shows that her parents named her Hester Sue."

At this the young boy who had been silently paying rapt attention to what the tall man did and said, suddenly blurted out, "Hester Sue? I ain't never heard nothin' like that before," and burst out laughing. The little girl also felt it was really funny and joined his guffaw. And under relaxed situations this type of response can often trigger much similar response from others so that there was a contagious round of happy participation.

Granny was the most animated one at the table. It struck her so funny that she couldn't stop with her ha-ha and reached to the man who was seated beside her and slapped him on the back and breathlessly said, "You rascal. I bet Major Colfax told you about me, didn't he?"

He nodded agreement but couldn't stop chuckling until he realized that the older woman's face was turning beet red and she began gasping for air. Gloria dashed across the room to Granny's purse and quickly obtained a capsule which when broken in the mouth brought relief almost momentarily. The medication was intended to relieve heart and respiration problems before they attained real emergency proportions.

Garth then provided a distraction by reaching into his pocket and fishing out change. "I haven't been properly introduced to the children." Gloria did this and after appropriate handshakes the man held out two shining copper pennies for both Mark and Maggie. He said, "I saw how you both helped Granny carry in the groceries. When I can, I like to show my appreciation to good children who try to help."

Granny saw how pleased they were and how they both gave big words of thanks to their unexpected benefactor. She now had her breath back and wanted to explain about the almost never heard Hester Sue name. She began by saying, "My birth papers name me as Hester Sue Bronson. The Bronson farm was about a mile east of the bridge across the river. My folks were both pretty old when I was born.

"I was in my thirties when I married Harold Brown whose folks had the farm about two miles west from ours. He worked at the lumber mill and he was about ten years older than me but all our days together were full of happy times. His private name for me was Sweet Sue and to me he was Handsome Harry. We had just one child, a boy we named Gerald. He fell in love with a very pretty gal, Virginia Dahlman, and wedding was in the books. Their firstborn is my sweetheart, Gloria.

"But shortly after Gloria's birth some very sad times came. The worst to me was a boiler explosion that killed my husband. The second was when that same year my folks died mainly from feeble old age within a few days of each other. But the only good thing about my folks passing was that we were sure there'd be no more sorrow or pain for them in their new home in Heaven. And as much as I hated the thought, my folks' will left everything to me which through the sale of their property meant this place was debt free and I had a little nest egg.

"My goodness! My memory gets jumbled. I forgot to mention that before Gerald's wedding he went to Michigan for a few days to meet Virginia's brothers and sisters who were all married and stayed there when her folks came here to teach school, but they went back after a couple years. When Gerald was there one of her brothers talked him into joining the Coast Guard and he did so a few years later though it caused him to be away from home too much.

"But the two of them were able to take a real honeymoon when Gloria was about nine. And Virginia, ever of poor health and frailty, was pregnant even though she'd been warned against it by her doctor. The hammer blow came when my son died trying to rescue folks in a sinking ship in Lake Michigan. Gloria's brother was born but the twin shocks to her mama ended her life. And I had a little girl who kept calling out to Granny about why. I still haven't the answers, but I still believe in the goodness of God."

It was a little after ten when the office phone rang and Gloria dashed to answer it. Those in the kitchen heard her accept the charges and then heard her exclaim "Frank!" before shutting the door. She wasn't on long before returning to the others with a disappointed look. She tersely explained, "They were supposed to be back from Omaha this evening but there have been some delays in the paperwork and also they had some unexpected car repairs needed. They all send their love to Granny and the kids and of course to me and Frank said we were not to worry over a five day delay. All businesses do have temporary setbacks but all is going good."

Garth said, "I'm looking forward to meeting your husband, Gloria, and the two helpers he has. And since I'm expecting to be here till the end of October, I also hope to meet your regular tenants, Granny."

The young wife responded, "Frank has a much diversified business he has named Miller Associates. Frank is an excellent salesman; friendly to everyone he ever meets. He particularly likes real estate deals, especially if starting up a new business or upgrading an old one is involved. He has a partnership with Jacob Ebner who is a whiz at drawing up contracts or agreements. He is also as capable as a CPA with financial matters. He is a rather quiet but not unfriendly and as good as many attorneys with legal knowledge."

She paused and Garth guessed her husband's extended absence really bothered her. He commented, "Maybe I'm mistaken, but I'm sure I heard there were three people involved in Miller Associates."

She replied, "There are three, but the other man is not a partner. He's called Burly Dodge. I think his actual name is Burton but he is a large and very strong man. He is a great handy man. He can do carpentry and plumbing and simple electrical repairs and he can fix most anything that might need fixing on an automobile like the Buick the business owns. But his best trait is how he loves children and might be ready to pulverize anyone who abuses them or mistreats a woman. The kids here call him Uncle Burly.

"They also call Jacob Ebner Uncle but he's much more reserved around kids although like your kinfolk I've tried to teach them respect for their elders. Officer Clancy O'Connor and his wife Dharma are included. They live in the apartment next to ours and in one of those strange coincidences I got acquainted with her when both of us were in the maternity ward at the same time. They had just moved in a month or so before that. And of all things our babies both arrived on the same day. But Margaret is about three hours older. Maureen and Maggie act just like sisters especially when they once in a while quarrel. But Maureen who calls me Auntie Glory is a flaming red head like her parents.

"Garth, here are your keys to your room and the outside entry. Mark, will you show Mr. Stone to his room and tell him the names of the upstairs roomers? I'm going to go with Dharma and our girls to the playground until lunch time. The Lutheran church is right around the corner from us and their playground is open to all kids. Their grave yard is behind the church. Later in the day when we're both free I'll see if I can personally introduce you to the other apartment people."

Mark lugged the man's bulky brief case up the stairs as Garth brought up the quite heavy big suitcase. The lad explained like a little professor about the ABC etcetera naming of the rooms. "Sir, you have the biggest single room, 2C. 2A is the one closest to Granny's end of the house and Nurse Ruth Hillman is in 2A. 2B is a double room and Uncle Burly and Uncle Jacob share it. And they have a phone. 2D right next to your room is vacant right now but 2E has Doctor Ronald Williams in and he has a phone, too. 2F is also vacant.

"My sister and Maggie and me live in Frank Miller's apartment 1D on the first floor and we both call him Daddy but he's not my daddy who I've only seen in one of

Granny's picture albums. We don't have a phone. In 1C are the O'Connor Family. He's a cop and me and Maggie call him Uncle Clancy and the Missus we call Auntie Dharma. Maggie and their girl, Maureen, are real pals. There's a phone in their apartment.

"In 1B are Mandy and William Cleveland. The three of us kids all call them Mr. or Mrs. cuz we ain't well acquainted. He works with records at the Court House and she's the Librarian. In 1A are Fred and Sandy Van Epps. Us kids call them Grandpa and Grandma cuz they're getting old and grey like Granny and they are always nice to us. Granny says they were teachers and now they're retired, whatever that means.

"One more thing. Granny said if you get a car there is plenty of parking space in the driveway. Uncle Clancy, Uncle Burly, and the Doctor all have cars but there's enough parking space for six. I guess that's everything for now. I hope you like your room."

Garth said, "Well thank you. I have been in many places where a tour guide would tell things of interest to the people gathered there, but you did just as good as any of them could. I really appreciate all you told me. Let me shake your hand and I intend to tell Granny and Mrs. Miller what a good tour guide you could be."

After the lad, obviously very happy from the man's man-to-man type hand shake and words of praise, went back downstairs, Garth put away his garments in the closet and dresser. He had then bathed in the nearest of the two bathrooms and put his soiled clothes in the convenient clothes basket in his room for later laundry attention for their modest fee. He had then opened his seaman-type trunks to make sure all his necessary equipment and supplies were safely stashed.

There was a timid rap on his door a little before noon. Mark said, "Granny sent this for you for now or later and she hopes you might have a little time to talk to her before the Sheriff comes to give you a ride." The lad handed over a plate laden with a cinnamon roll wrapped in wax paper with toothpicks preventing the glaze from sticking.

The man soon picked up his brief case, now lightly loaded with just necessary papers, and went down to the pleasant office where the spry woman made sure he was comfortable and apologized for not offering him lunch since she knew he was invited out. Her custom was to call younger folks sons and daughters even if there was no blood relationship.

"Son, your mother died when you were little and I never heard what become of you until Major Colfax sent me a letter a few days ago saying you worked in his department of the government and you'd be teaching here for a few weeks. So I want to tell you a few things what have happened here since your father left here after your mother's death. We only had that four room school house with two grades in each room and weren't you in second grade?"

"That's right, Granny. The farm was losing more money each year and there was a big mortgage, so Dad sold the farm and all the tools and furniture to pay off the debt and we went to live with a cousin of his in upper Michigan. Dad shipped all the things we needed and he included all the books I needed to finish my eight grades so I could pass the final exam and get my certificate. He made me study every night no matter where we were. And him and I went hunting or fishing almost every day and what we got helped keep my second cousin's wife and three kids fed through the winter. And that's how I got trained to properly use a firearm."

Granny picked up the talk, "Did you know that when the wagon train came here, there were about 100 folks and about 18 wagons? They was mostly folks what wanted to have a farming community and most of them was from Michigan, Indiana, and Illinois. They weren't taken in by the talk of how the 49ers was getting rich and they came in 1851. There was five families; Stillwell, Colfax, Strait, Brown, and Stone. About 40 were Stillwell kin, 50 or so of the Colfax and Strait and the Browne and Stone about a half dozen each. Son, you're the only male Stone in town now and my grandson Mark and me is the only Browns what are left.

"Before your father moved away with you there was just one teacher and a one room school house where the bigger kids would help teach the little kids. But not many went past the third grade and I'm proud of how your dad helped you get your eighth grade certificate. As the town grew the number of students got so big we built a kindergarten through 12th grade school and named it the Franklin School after that wise man from colonial days.

"Now since the Stillwell group led that first wagon train and since this area seemed ideal the first settlers decided it was fitting it be called Stillwell. And this county was named after the town and it is the county seat. Well, with more and more folks moving into the area, there had to be a hospital and when it was built it was thought proper to honor Florence Nightingale so our county hospital is named the Nightingale Hospital. And it's modern and even has X-Ray machines."

Garth said, "Granny, I do believe you're like one of those encyclopedias. But I have a faint memory of my father and me going to my mother's funeral in a small church across the river and could you tell me if it is still meeting?"

"They're still going strong doing God's work and they're still in the same place doing it and the flock has nearly doubled. It's still called the Grace Memorial Chapel. The biggest churches right in town are the oldest church named the First Baptist, the Good Shepherd Lutheran Church around the corner, Our Lady of Mercy Catholic Church, the Calvin Reformed Church, and the Wesleyan Church. There are also eight or ten small gatherings. There's also Mount Sinai Synagogue. I would guess over half the population of adults and children would claim membership at a place of worship but a lot of people don't go too regular. And while you're in town I'd be real happy if you came to the Lutheran services with us and get acquainted with our Pastor Herman Michaels and his wife Bertha."

"Thank you for the invitation. I have made it a habit to worship whenever it's possible on the Sabbath. My father and I sought out church wherever we were in our travels. And I'm sure I won't have many Sunday duties while I'm here."

Granny smiled broadly and said, "And after church I won't take no as an answer to you being at my Sunday dinner. But there might have to be an hour or so delay so Gloria and me can do the finishing touches."

He heartily agreed but only on the condition he would be allowed to take her out for dinner in the near future. She said, "That would be a treat. But let's not talk about it cuz I got a few more things I wanted to mention. There are a lot of descendants from that original wagon train who are prominent citizens. I'll just name some. Major Reginald Colfax who moved to D.C. to work for the government but he has relatives here yet. Mayor Bernie Stillwell. His cousin Judge Nehemiah Stillwell whose son James is an attorney. Sheriff Caleb Strait. And there are others on the school board or hospital board and some who have money in various enterprises around the county."

About then the Sheriff's car pulled up and the horn was heard. "Thanks so much, Granny, for useful information and also for the cinnamon roll I'll be enjoying before I go to bed. See you later."

About five he arrived at Swede's Place down the block from the Police Station. He was dressed in his semi-official uniform he usually wore when on duty. It was composed of a dark tan three piece suit, a light tan shirt, a brown tie, well shined black shoes and a western style very light tan Stetson. But what identified it as a lawman's garb was a U.S. Marshal's badge in front of his heart and a noticeable bulge of his holster under the deliberately roomy jacket. When he was too warm for his jacket, he could shed it and wear the badge on his vest.

Swede was the common name for the proprietor, Nels Dahlgren, whose wife Sonja was in charge of the kitchen. The couple's daughter, Heidi was the Hostess and in charge of the waitresses. The trio saw Garth through the plate glass window as he came to the entrance and gave him a warm welcome into the already filling dining room. The Sheriff had earlier instructed the young man of a possibly hazardous situation and also told him how some information had been shared with Nels who in early years had been part of a trio of buddies who hunted and fished together as opportunity arose. Garth's father had often gone with the two men as their careers aimed toward law and food.

After the terse introduction Swede said to Sonja that maybe she ought to go back into the kitchen before the Saturday evening Family Time had a rush. Then he said to Heidi it would be best if Gloria would only be the lawman's waitress since there was some information for her and the two could use the small private dining room usually only used for politicians secret talks.

Heidi told the Marshal that Gloria was already there and seemed to be very nervous. The young woman met him just inside the small room and pointed out a pitcher of iced tea and a carafe of steaming hot coffee. She said, "It's pretty warm in here so if you'd rather have a cold beverage I'll pour some for you but Granny taught me years ago to stick with hot coffee."

"Mrs. Miller, we're of one mind about that. And I'm quite hungry but before we order I have to put some first things first. And I'll also put my hat on the rack while you pour and it's black and no sugar for mine."

She looked intently at his badge and noticed the bulge at his hip under his suit coat. "Marshal Stone, since we are supposed to have a private chat, could you please call me Gloria?" She tried to act nonchalant but failed.

He replied, "Only if in non-public chats you call me Garth. Okay?" He was well aware that except for Heidi's silvery blond hair and this married woman's light brown, the two were almost of identical appearance, even as to height and their figures. The flour-specked lady in Granny's hand-me-down housework dress with wind-ravaged hair was a completely different image than this chic almost sophisticated woman in a fashionable dress and shoes and a frilly apron.

He unbuttoned his suit coat and removed a legal size manila envelope and handed it to her across the table. The heading was Mrs. Frank Miller which was followed in parentheses by Gloria Miller. The woman tried to read the fine print on the document and her eyes became tearful as from fright. "Is this a warrant for my arrest? You're taking me to jail? What about my children?"

"Whoa! This isn't a warrant. Those Latin words are favorite means of lawyers who write these things for the Judge. This document means that the Sheriff's department and me as a Government appointed Marshal are ordered to give you protective custody, as much as is needed so that you and your kids are to be kept safe. But why in the world would you ever think you would be arrested? The Sheriff said you have always been a completely law-abiding good citizen just like Granny."

"I think my brain must have really been muddled. But some of the other girls I know about my age I think are jealous. Heidi and I have been best of friends since grade school. And even better after my mother died and I tried to do anything I could to earn a few coins to help to take care of Mark. Nels let me come in and sweep and do little chores and Heidi is a year older than me and she would show me how to do things and we would also do stuff together. Now she often lets me wear some of her clothes because my husband's business is still struggling and we can't afford better stuff yet. So jealous people might tell tales and make it look like I stole stuff. But I never have."

He very seriously replied, "I am totally sure of your complete innocence. And I must comment that both Heidi and you look very nice. And I will try to explain just what is happening but right at the moment I would prefer to shift our attentions to eating. The delicious cinnamon roll was my entire breakfast and Aunt Ellen served her very tasty recipe of chicken noodle soup and gave us Jell-O with fruit cocktail in it for dessert. She told me she had been working on Uncle Caleb to lose a few pounds and apologized for the lighter lunch. So would you be able to eat a meal with me, or have you already eaten?"

His entire facial expression told her that what he had said was the gospel truth and she relaxed but also admitted she was actually hungrier than she had realized. "Mister, uh, I mean Garth, it seems like both of us didn't eat much today. I just had a tiny helping of oatmeal when the rest of us ate breakfast and then the roll and after we came back from the playground I just gobbled a slice of bread smeared with peanut butter. And Swede and Sonja told me to let you know that whatever the two of us get is all on the house for us tonight and they said I would get my regular pay."

He examined the menu and asked, "Don't they serve regular big meals? All I see are sandwiches, soup, and desserts."

She said, "This is mostly a lunchroom with a separate room with pool and card tables where liquor may be served to adults only. But the biggest attraction is great breakfasts served any time and they're listed on the back of the menu. If you're really hungry I recommend the Lumberjacks feast.

Beverage, orange juice, grits with gravity if you wish, fried potatoes, ham, eggs, toast and jam, and a donut or Danish. For me it will be juice, a few flapjacks, some pork sausage links, and maybe a donut."

He nodded and smiled his agreement and she scurried to place their order. After she returned and sat down opposite him he said, "Most of the Stone family parents expected a return of thanks to God before eating as I'm certain you and Granny do so would you do like me and bow your head and clasp your hands before the food even comes?"

She smiled at him and did as he asked. He used the little prayer he had been taught as a little boy. "We thank you Heavenly Father for what we now partake and ask you to help us be good for Jesus' sake. Amen." She echoed his amen, and felt much less stressed over all the questions in her mind. He told her she really had nothing to worry about and he would give her detailed information after they ate.

"Gloria, you will ride home in an auto when we're all done. The office has cars available for all the deputies and a couple extras for urgent situations. Since I will need to be travelling around the town and the county for various works I need to do, I was assigned a somewhat old but well-kept two door model A Ford. I never thought I'd become a teacher or lecturer when I agreed to serve as a Marshal, but that's a primary part of the month and a half I'll be here.

"You see, I've been learning about shooting since I was very little and as my skill increased I won a number of trophies and awards in competition and I was also able to help the police in Chicago to aid government agents in shutting down rum-runners and bootleggers. So my boss thought it would be helpful to law enforcement agencies, state game wardens, and even school children and civic groups if I boosted knowledge of the law and particularly helped officers and hunters regarding gun safety and good marksmanship."

She was impressed even more by him than before. She rather shyly asked if he might perhaps allow her to get a few groceries on their way back to Granny's and he informed her he also needed a few personal items. It was only a few minutes before a buzzer rang by the door to their room and she quickly opened it to move the serving cart to the table which she quickly set.

They were both hungrier than they had realized and neither said much as they concentrated on their bountiful banquet. As they were slowly finishing the last of their meals he commented, "Wow! That was great. But could my Danish be wrapped to take home? I'll have it in the morning but the roll later tonight."

She cleared their table except for the coffee container and moved the cart back to the kitchen with instructions that both of them wished to take their pastries home later.

He was silent for a couple of minutes before beginning to speak to her. "Gloria, there is a good reason you and Granny and the children are needed to be under protective custody. Miller Associates was approached by some of the people who had worked with the mobs during Prohibition and informed by them that their cooperation was mandatory in Omaha if they expected to run their own business in the city. Frank and Jacob had sent Burly on an errand so he was not an immediate hearer of what was wanted. Since betting parlors could not be worked in by out-of-towners, those illegal places couldn't use them.

"But there are two other illegal activities where they could fit in. One of them was the Numbers Racket. People would pay small amounts such as dimes or quarters and much like lottery winners received considerably bigger winnings than their tiny ticket price. But the numerous sellers of the tickets got a percentage of their sales. However those running the Numbers games kept the fattened lion's share.

"The other and much worse lawlessness involved the Protection Insurance. In this were people who were husky and mostly well-mannered and well dressed. These collectors or enforcers of a gang that controlled a sizable district would get money from all the small business folk. Now you didn't have to get their insurance but if you didn't, bad things began to happen. Store windows got broken late at night and unexplained accidents happened. Most of the police were honest but a few corrupt politicians saw to it that officers that looked the other way when bad things happened seemed too often to get anonymous gifts.

"Is your husband a bit outspoken and quick to say what's on his mind?"

"As a matter of fact that's the way he is. But isn't that how most good salesmen are? And Frank isn't afraid to tell people what he thinks is best for them."

"So he was quick to tell the two goons, that's what I call them, to quit annoying honest folks and if they came again he was calling the Police commissioner and also getting a lawyer and suing them. And after midnight two other gorillas, that's what else I call them, waited until the apartment was quiet and the lights off and smashed their way in. The lights came on immediately and Burly crashed into them and threw both of them down the stairs before they even had a chance to use their baseball bats.

"This time the police came fast and there was an immediate ride in the paddy wagon to waiting cells. I'll condense this now. The following day the boss of the first two enforcers came with them to the Deli and brazenly told Frank and Jacob that it wouldn't matter if they did sue for their business card gave the address of Granny's place where Frank's wife and kids were and how awful if there were any accidents there."

The woman's lips began to quiver and her eyes were getting moist as she said with a tremulous voice, "I'm not scared for me, but what about Granny and the kids. And I don't know what I'd do if my husband was…." She could not finish her words.

"Don't fret or be afraid. Both Frank and Jacob have begun carrying 38's when they're in dangerous situations and when there was a threat implied to any of you they were quick to have Burly or a witness call the Police Commissioner's office and also apply a citizen's arrest at gunpoint until the police arrived. Thugs usually think they know it all but in truth many of them are pretty stupid. You see after the raids and such regarding Prohibition in major cities, every person thought to be involved had their pictures sent to the big towns and state police. And in many cases, including the person who made the threats, there were outstanding warrants for failure to obey court orders or to skip away from bail requirements.

"I admire how the Miller Associates make a habit of informing the local authorities whenever they begin to open up a new area for business. And I had to chuckle when I heard that Burly whom some have said has iron fists, has taken to carrying a stout walking stick with a substantial brass knob at the top. I can hardly wait to meet that trio of brave businessmen.

"I'm so glad the O'Connors live in the next apartment to you. I haven't met them yet but Uncle Caleb has told me about them. Deputy Clancy has been a cop for over ten years and amazingly Dharma has almost as many years of experience. They lived in a small rowdy town I forget the name of in Arizona. As a young man her dad, Mickey, worked as a bouncer in a saloon and it was soon found that he could quickly bring back peace and quiet during bar brawls.

"But the small town had no lawman and things kept getting worse so that finally the town council held an election and only Mickey ran. But when he needed a deputy, no one wanted to be involved so he hired Dharma and she was almost as good a fracas stopper as he had been plus she had often hunted and was competent with firearms. One of the little jokes at the station is that Clancy's girl Maureen has a pistol packing mama. And aren't all three kids being tended tonight until you get home by Dharma and Clancy? Doesn't that lessen any worries you might have?"

"Garth, it's like a weight off my shoulders. It's just like God is letting me know that He knows about everything and has planned to send folks even when they don't know He sent them. And since I'm thinking about God's goodness to all of us, I'm looking forward to worship tomorrow to see what God has given to Rev. Michaels for us. You haven't had to change your plans have you?"

"Are you kidding? I want the Pastor to feed my soul and Granny to feed my belly. And also remember that since Clancy and his family go to the Catholic Mass, it behooves me to be the protector for all of you tomorrow. And I'm gonna bring the Ford up near the entrance cuz it looks like rain might be coming."

As soon as she was in the car he asked her if she minded if he drove to the Standard Oil gas station at the south end of town to fill the gas tank and then to the grocery store near Granny's for any necessary things. She did not often have the opportunity to ride in an automobile and it was a special treat for her that her chauffeur was a U.S. Marshal sent by the government.

He inquired about her friendship with Heidi and she literally gushed about what a great pal she was and how she was always looking for good things to do for others. "She teaches some of the younger Sunday school kids and takes some of her free time to read stories to kids at the library. She'll go out of her way to visit some of the elderly in nursing homes who seldom have any visitors and she is so quick to visit folks who are shut-ins, and how cheerful and friendly she is to the folks who stop in at Swede's. She and Dharma are a couple of my very best friends. When Frank is away and I get gloomy and sad, either of them can break my blue mood."

After Garth parked the car, he carried her bag of groceries to her apartment door and upon hearing voices within before her door was opened he wished her a good night's rest and excused himself claiming he still had quite a few documents to read before he slept. He also had in mind to nibble on that cinnamon roll.

In the morning Garth made a small pot of coffee on the room's hot plate and had his Danish from Swede's for a quick breakfast. He thought about the propriety of wearing his official uniform to church and realized that many officers went to services in their varied houses of worship and were ready to go directly from the church to their duties. He was a bit concerned about carrying his weapon but once he met the Reverend, the Man of God assured that it would be acceptable.

The sermon title was God is Love and True Love is of God. The minister clearly showed that the Lord Jesus had taught that all of the commandments were summed up by loving God and others. Then he emphasized that over years in the ministry he had come to the conclusion that a lack of true love was the main reason for most mental and spiritual disorders and in his mind the most heart-breaking of all was loneliness.

"God let it be known from the beginning that marriage was the greatest antidote for the inner emptiness of being alone. He stressed the importance of going out of your way to demonstrate by loving deeds to others in their state of being lonesome for God. This was at the very heart of God's plan for bringing lost souls home. So since God is love, be showing this to all those around and thus fulfill Jesus' plan for your life."

During the entire service Garth sat in the right rear pew from which place he could with a glance observe the entrance to the sanctuary so that if anyone entered who seemed suspicious, he would immediately be alert to the expressions of the ushers and those to whom the folks they sat with did not seem to know them. Granny and Gloria sat near the front. The Dahlgrens came in together and each greeted Garth before going up the right aisle to be seated in the pew behind Granny's bunch.

There seemed to the Marshal that there was a very reverent and friendly atmosphere to the sacred room and also very little whispering once the service got started. He also liked how children up into sixth grade were released after the offering and preliminaries to attend their own children's church led by the pastor's wife Bertha assisted by an usher and a high school teenager. He was sure they were very safe in the fellowship room in the basement.

He had wondered about Sunday school but the only other service was in the evening on the Lord's Day. But this was preceded by young people's meetings. However Tuesday evening was set aside for Bible classes for all ages and followed by cookies and beverage. And of course coming events were told.

Heidi and Gloria gabbed happily on the big church porch and then Sonja led her husband over to Garth and almost demanded that he be their guest for dinner in their apartment above their restaurant on any convenient evening except Saturday when they stayed open later or on Sundays when they were closed and often chose to attend the evening service. He agreed he'd get in touch with her as soon as he had his schedule in order.

But before any more conversation, Granny had corralled the Dahlgrens and quickly explained, "When we were planning our Sunday dinner, we were expecting Gloria's hubby and his helpers and didn't know they'd be delayed. And I hate to be stuck with lots of leftovers so it would be perfect if the three of you will join us and the Marshal."

It was immediately a done deal. The only irregularity was that Garth first changed into casual clothes and chose a seat where he had good eyes on the entrances, even though they were bolted, and a separate chair was close to him with his gun belt hanging on within easy reach.

He was absolutely certain those under his "protective custody" were as safe as was humanly possible. And also Clancy brought him a note from the Sheriff stating that J. Edgar Hoover's organization was wreaking havoc with organized crime tactics and threats. The Federal agents were having a good harvest of wrong-doers who surprisingly were in greater scrutiny relating to income tax evasion or failure to declare all their income.

Garth passed on the good news that he and Clancy would not need to continue being concerned about danger to those protected. And then after the too delicious pie for dessert and a round of praise to Granny and Gloria he said, "It seems like too beautiful an afternoon to just sit around the house and be dozing off. So I would be very happy to have Granny and the Millers go for a ride with me and show me where some of the places are that I've been told about.

"I would particularly appreciate it if Hester Sue would sit in front and be my tour guide." This brought on a round of giggles but more subdued than the first episode had been.

Granny maintained a more sober demeanor than the first episode and spoke rather sternly, "Young man, you will either call me Granny, or I will call you Buster." And then her resolve dissolved and she grinned and chuckled lightly.

Granny was a good tour guide and directed him to the places she had told him about the previous day. She was also quick to show him the route to the Grace Memorial Chapel just across the river north of the train depot. She explained as they arrived that the building was more than twice the size it had been when Garth had as a preschooler attended his mother's funeral.

There was an auto parked near the parsonage next door to the church and a man who fit the old memory of the one who presided over the service and had so much good to say about his mother back then rushed over to the car to greet them and to invite them in. When told how he hadn't really changed he had replied, "Marshal Stone that was my dad you heard. He is now retired and after I finished seminary and was ordained, my wife and I were sure the call they extended to me was the call of God to follow my father's footsteps. And God has over and over shown us the power of His gospel to change lives."

The travelers also went down to where the Stone farm had been and then to where Granny had once lived. Everyone enjoyed the pleasant afternoon. After they arrived home, there soon came a call from Heidi's mother Sonja with an insistent invitation to Garth to come to a smorgasbord on Monday evening. They met in the restaurant with a number of Swede's other relatives. And afterwards the man was easily beguiled to take Heidi to the Majestic Theater in Crawford to watch Clark Gable in It Happened One Night.

Whenever Garth was given assignments his meals, lodging, and incidentals were provided for. But when others provided for these things he could with permission and clear conscience divert funds. He and Heidi both enjoyed the twenty minute drives and he was impressed by her scope of knowledge. And both of them had common ground in the matters of faith and ethics. He was not too sure about her political convictions, but his also were a bit vague. Their common ground was a firm belief in democracy and the Constitution. He had a strong feeling that they might very likely develop strong friendships but what their futures held was not something he dared speculate on. But he certainly had to admit he enjoyed her company.

The man pondered long that evening before his sleep came on the words Rev. Michaels had spoken about the problem of loneliness. He realized he knew too much about that but always offered a confident attitude even when he sometimes felt empty. And then he thought about Gloria Miller. She seemed like such a good mother and so cheerful. But he also admitted to himself that for a woman to have a husband he guessed to be about twenty five or maybe even thirty years older than her seemed to bode much trouble for them as time marched on.

And then he thought about Heidi and how pleasant that evening had been. At the least it had been a highpoint in his often ho-hum existence. A Marshal's life way seem exciting, but most of the time it was dull routine. But he realized he knew more about lonely hours than most folks knew. His imagination kept going back to how great it could be if God saw fit to cause his path to cross the path of the right person for him.

He finally prayed thanking Jesus who had been his own Shepherd and especially asked the Lord to shelter Gloria and her kids and her husband and also to protect Heidi. From this he ended up asking a blanket protection over all the folks he had already met. And then he slept like a baby.

CHAPTER TWO

Gloria told her brother Mark on Monday not to say anything to anyone that it would be his tenth birthday anniversary on Saturday, a week since Marshal Stone's arrival. "Sometimes children like to keep hinting to be sure no one forgets, and when Daddy and your two uncles get here from Omaha, they're sure to have lots on their minds. But the way Uncle Jacob keeps track of dates and dollars, I'm sure you'll not be forgotten. And there is a very good possibility that Granny and I won't forget either."

The dusty Buick with almost equally dusty trio arrived late in the afternoon Thursday and they quickly carried mysterious packages to their lodging places. They were all assailed with the appetite tempting smell of one of Granny's well known stews and a smell suspiciously like apple pie. It did not take the trio long to give affectionate greetings to the old lady, the wife, and two very excited children.

Gloria had heard the toots of the horn as Burly had pulled into the driveway and she had literally run from the Miller apartment to fly to the entry to embrace her husband. "Frank, I missed you so much and I was so scared something bad had happened to the three of you." She could hardly stop hugging and kissing him and telling him how much she loved him and he responded similarly.

Maggie rushed right past Uncle Jacob to grab Uncle Burly around the legs and was picked up by him to hug her and call her his little sweetie pie. Mark was alert enough to first greet his daddy and Uncle Jacob with hugs and handshakes and then rushed over to the big man who medium sized friends nicknamed a gentle giant. The lad also was hoisted up next to the girl he always considered his little sister.

And then the trio of dusty men were all glad to clean up and shave and don clean clothes so they could get the best meal they'd had in many days. As they finished their meal at Granny's dining room table, the Marshal came back from his supper and Gloria summoned him in to meet her husband and his partners.

Frank vigorously shook hands and strongly offered thanks for the lawman's available protection in case it might have been needed. "Everywhere we've gone the men of the law have made us welcome and watched out for our safety and also often give directions to find places. I don't know what this land would be like without people who are determined to keep it safe and fight against illegal activities. I include the military in my appreciation."

The second man he shook hands with was Burly who was also quick to thank him and say that the thing he hated most of all was anyone who would harm children, women, the elderly, or disabled. "I only met you two minutes ago but I hope we can be good friends and if there is anything I can do to help you, be quick to let me know."

The third man immediately apologized that he had on snug gloves such as physicians wear, but Garth shook with him, yet gently. "Thank you. I had bad chemical burns a few years back and the appearance of my hands tends to make many folks nervous about touching them lest there be a rash or something they could get. And also I have to be careful about what I handle because I have to sometimes use a salve on them. And my thanks to you also."

Later on when Garth thought about his first encounter he warned himself to be careful about drawing too many conclusions too soon. Frank's diction and carefully thought out words made him think of politicians and how easily they can make appealing presentations. But Frank was first of all a salesman and that ought to be considered and not allow any too rapid jumps to unproved assumptions.

Big Burly affected him the way Granny or Swede or Heidi or Mrs. Miller did at first encounter. Garth immediately liked the man and was sure he could trust him. He could recall a number of times when it took no more than a few seconds for a conviction to come over him that he and the other person were on common ground; that they had a basic belief in the ethics of Christ.

He was a tiny bit nervous about Jacob Ebner but had no clue as to why he felt that way. Perhaps it was the stronger than necessary attention called to his gloved hands. A good lawman is not to form strong opinions without facts and if a man often called attention to a problem, however small, there might have been in his past some big hurts or slights which he wished to avoid.

After Garth left, the children went to the O-Connor apartment to play some silly games with Auntie Dharma and Maureen until Depute Clancy got off duty. This left five to sip coffee at the table until Burly excused himself and went up to get a wrapped gift he handed to Granny to unwrap after Frank spoke.

"Ladies, even though the country is recovering from the Great Depression, there is still much hardship for way too many families. Therefore many community groups such as churches and civic organizations have opened up places where folks can sell used things they can get by without, in order to gain a little money. We did a little shopping at some of these centers but our hearts were so moved by the plight of so many that we always made it a habit to pay a little more than was the asking price.

"Religious people would say we were tithing because we made it a practice to give them a tenth more than they asked for, thus helping our fellow citizens at least a little bit. So dear lady, when we saw this lap quilt we immediately thought of how you often like to sit and rock on the front porch under the roof in case it rains. And it's getting so when the sun goes down it's getting chilly and you can keep your feet and legs cozy."

The ladies opened the package and literally loved the quilt which had almost no signs of wear and was a true work of art with many colors that made it resemble a verdant flower garden. Granny was momentarily speechless and could only tell them thanks and that they hadn't needed to spend so much for her gift.

Burly said, "Ever since I first met you, you've been forever doing good for everyone around you. We all want you to know you're one in a million."

Burly insisted that Gloria and Frank go to their apartment and let him and Jacob assist Granny with dishes. It had been noticed that the children were quite tired and Frank was beginning to show signs of extreme fatigue to the point where he was almost nodding off and his hands were quivering. In their apartment the man quickly gathered wife and kids around their table to tell them about an encounter he'd had with an elderly Indian medicine man of unknown tribe.

"I met him at a pow-wow in a park. I've his name and address but his name was so hard for me to say he made me call him Pete. I learned from him that he had spent most of his life practicing what he called natural medicine where all the remedies are made from combinations of herbs and spices. He told me his special tonic would calm my nerves when I got all worked up over business stresses or if I wasn't sleeping well. Nothing in it requires a prescription.

"I thought at first it was just another way for Pete to make money but he insisted I try it out using a small free sample bottle. And he said that it could be used by most people of any age without any bothersome side effects. But of course doses had to be based on the body size of the user. To my amazement I began to have better nights of sleep and less brain strain over business problems. The tonic also seemed to keep me from getting upset over things that used to bother me much more. It even helps my digestion.

"So I became a regular mail order customer of Medicine Man Peter's Tonic. And didn't a carton come addressed to me at this address a few days ago?"

Gloria said, "A carton was delivered a few days ago and I put it up on the shelf in your closet. It was kind of heavy and I think it was full of bottles. I was curious but it was addressed to you and I thought it might be for your business."

"Indirectly it is for it helps me do a better job. And I've been seeing articles in magazines where doctors say that good food with all the vitamins you need will do the kind of things Peter's Tonic does for me. And since I'm so sure of how much good it's done for me, I'm hoping you and the kids will let me give you some of it. After all, we've all heard how naturally grown herbs and spices are good for all of us."

Frank continued, "But before we warm glasses of milk and add tonic for the kids, I want them to watch you open gifts I got for you. I'll admit the gifts were not bought in an expensive store and were used as I had mentioned regarding the quilt for Granny, for our business still has to be cautious about funds, but when I saw the items, I knew they were meant to be yours for the lady who had to give them up for sale had her initial on them, a capital Gee which could mean Gloria."

Within the package was first of all a face-sized hand held mirror, followed by a luxurious hair brush accompanied by a quality comb. These three items all had her initial on them and were trimmed with sterling silver. Finally there was a compact which hinged opened to a small mirror and a powder puff and powder. As Gloria saw these thoughtful and beautiful gifts the young woman was overwhelmed and tears filled her eyes as she threw her arms around her man to kiss him and tell him she loved him and couldn't thank him enough. She told him it made her feel like a millionaire.

Both children told the man they called Daddy that they loved him too and he replied by saying how happy he was and how he had never been happier and that no man could have a better wife or family. And then he gave a small glass of warm milk to Maggie who had napped that afternoon. Mark received a larger glass. The little girl had a half teaspoon of tonic and Mark a teaspoon.

Both children went quickly through their pre-bed routines and were very drowsy. The man then suggested that he and his wife get ready for bed, she in the silk night gown he had earlier brought her and he in his pajamas. He then had her sit on the little bench in front of the mirror with her new mirror in her hand at her dresser. She thought it was wonderful that two mirrors made it possible to see all around her hair. No one but Frank had ever seen her without a robe over her gown.

And then he gently brushed her hair and whispered to her about how he had never before ever loved another such a graceful and attractive woman. Finally they both had glasses of juice with a tablespoon of tonic in hers but more than double the amount in his.

She slept more soundly than ever but was nonetheless vaguely aware of his physical nearness and attention to her. She over slept in the morning as did the children and she was also aware of minor aches and pains she attributed to how her husband often tossed and turned in his sleep. But she was also pleased that while she was still waking up the man had made a pot of coffee and also made cocoa for the children. The pungent odor of strong coffee aroused her enough to get her up and into her robe and then into the kitchen to make pancakes.

After breakfast Mark headed off to school and Maggie went to see Auntie Dharma and her playmate Maureen. It was not until they were alone that Frank told his wife that she would attend the presentation of business changes which were intended to financially protect her in the unlikely event of unforeseen tragedy.

At about one Friday afternoon a gathering of folks came together in the office of Attorney James Stillwell, son of Judge Nehemiah Stillwell, to prepare a Trust. He requested it be informal and all use first names until documents would need full signatures. Granny, Gloria, Frank, Burly, and Jacob were present but only Gloria had no prior knowledge of what was expected to transpire. Also present were Garth, Mayor Bernard Stillwell (an uncle of the lawyer) and Sheriff Caleb Strait.

James made the presentation and in plain English answered any questions. "Granny came to me about a strong will which would turn over all her property and assets to Gloria, who is only 18 and would not have much say until she is 21. But that would require the appointment of court-approved supervision. Now Gloria would at 21 have a legal claim to 50% of all Frank owns and controls. But the simplest way of handling estates and such is through an appropriate trust."

Then the Attorney explained how folks could have their assets better protected, particularly when there might be a death of a relative. He explained what profits really were and how under a trust all parties involved would have equal protection.

He continued, "If all parties involved agree, both Miller Associates and Hester's property would be involved. But there would be a number of Trustees to administer the new trust. These Trustees would have a vote based on the assets which they have. Their titles could be indicative of their interest. Frank is to continue as President of that business, Jacob as Treasurer/Accountant, and Burly for Security/Maintenance. Frank will have majority vote since he put up most of the seed money when they started. Jacob also invested a lesser amount and would have a smaller vote. Burly would have a small minority vote to compensate him for all the work he put in.

"It looks like Hester's vote will be larger than Frank's and her title might be that of Proprietress. Her vote currently will be larger than Frank's since her assets are larger. And I mustn't forget about Gloria who at age 21 will step into her grandmother's trusteeship. And also Frank has agreed that she will own half of his Miller Associates share at that time and will be Vice President.

"Now to guarantee that there will never be any question about funds or procedures followed before Gloria's legal age, there will be two additional unpaid Trustees who will act to oversee and advise. These two undisputed men of good legal knowledge and upstanding moral characters are our Honorable Mayor Bernard Stillwell and Sheriff Caleb Strait. At their request all financial records including any information in safe deposit boxes will be available.

"Two more things before we begin signing documents. As you know, my father Nehemiah Stillwell is a Federal Judge and he carefully went over all these papers and is in full agreement that this is a very good plan for all of you. He also is a good friend of Marshal Stone's employer, Major Reginald Colfax, who was very glad to hear that Garth would be sitting in as an extra witness."

At this point Garth wished to seek additional information. "James, if Jacob is going to help Granny with her bookkeeping, will she still have to send out checks for phone and water and electricity and coal for the furnace etcetera?"

The lawyer pointed at Jacob and gestured that he answer that one. Jacob turned his chair to better face Garth and said, "Granny has done a great job with her money management and ledger but she has already told me that if the Trust is agreed to, she would be more than happy to pay the small sum I suggested to do all of it for her. She said she has done it long enough and would just as soon get a professional money handler to relieve her of that chore."

Granny chuckled and said, "Amen to that. I get sick of numbers."

Jacob was usually serious, but he actually chuckled and said, "Just so the Sheriff doesn't come breathing down my neck when I'm counting out the money."

By this time, despite the continual work of a good fan and the open windows, it was getting quite warm in the meeting room and James had his secretary bring in pitchers of iced tea and lemonade to refresh all those present. She included a platter of small cookies to munch on during the signing of the numerous papers. She also was a state registered Notary and her crimping stamp was valid proof she had witnessed each signing by all of the aforementioned signers.

All of the people present were glad to rise and walk around the room after the signing and had a chance to chat a bit. Frank made it a point to hug his wife and give her a light kiss on her cheek. She could hardly believe what had just transpired and he softly told her it was because he loved her so much and wanted to do the most he could to show how concerned he was for her future should any tragedies arise.

Frank then moved her with him to Garth and said, "My wife and I want to give you our thanks for lending to my family the security of your protection should it have been necessary. Oh. James wants us to be seated again so I as President of our Association can bring one more important item before the Trustees.

"A few months back Jacob and I were telling Granny about a couple of home-based businesses we assisted a couple of widows to start. Neither widow had the necessary assets to put their skills into a small business. They required us to withhold any vital information from anyone else. The one woman was great at baking all kinds of delicacies and hoped she could somehow begin a small bakery and include a coffee house. We were able to negotiate a small bank loan and also were able to do the contracting so that a cozy shop was quickly added to the front of her home and she is beginning to show a modest but steadily increasing profit which is rapidly paying off her loan and giving her a bit more income.

"The other widow was a great seamstress and had been able to make a bit by sewing up garments. She also had hopes of more room to work and a dream that she could sell fabric, needles and thread and such, and patterns. We were able to help her add a substantial wing on her house and at present she actually has a part time assistant to sew and sell with her. Again with our help the woman got a loan and Burly supervised the contractor's crew. Our business acumen and their skills worked together to improve their financial conditions."

Granny said, "Gloria and me liked the idea of this and she put the idea on her wish list for some far-off distant time. But when Frank and Jacob had a private talk, I agreed that I would go along with the whole idea but not break any of it to Gloria. So I signed some papers with them to at least check into it all and it sure looks like it's possible. We even came up with a name for it, Gloria's Shoppe. And everything is set to begin as soon as the spring thaws set in."

At this point Jacob stepped up to a small easel and folded back the cloth cover. There were several photos of little home-based sewing businesses to show some of the possibilities. Then there were preliminary architect's sketches and a possible layout indicating a coffee counter, a dressing room, a ladies rest room, and possible locations of counters, racks, etc.

As soon as comments were made, questions asked, and explanations extended, Burly asked for a chance to speak. "Granny and Gloria, I've only known both of you for a few years, but I gotta say how impressed I am by the sewing work you've both done. And I agree that this town couldn't have a better thing added than what Jacob showed us. I'm 100% for this. I can't see how we could have two better ladies involved."

The young wife was totally flabbergasted that such planning and preparation had already taken place and she had secretly hoped that in the future she and her grandmother could become partners in such an endeavor. She asked her husband if she could share this wonderful idea with her best friends Heidi and Dharma of whom she was sure both could at least for the present not tell the idea around. Her husband agreed that at least until more details were worked out it would be best to keep it hush hush from any others but them.

Garth went over to Granny and reminded her of the promise he'd made earlier about taking her out for supper and she hadn't forgotten. He said, "Would you mind terribly if I made this an occasion a threesome. If so I'll take Heidi along and the two of you can make sure my table manners are correct."

She replied with a poor imitation of a stern expression, "Young man, are you trying to trifle with my affections?"

He tried to mimic her facial expression and answered, "Madam, I would never trifle with your affection. There is no grander lady in the world as far as I'm concerned than you. But I am hoping you will be there for my protection against the advances of the fair maiden." And the Marshal was in no way able to be stern the way he could easily be while dealing with law breakers and he couldn't keep himself from laughing which prompted a gentle laugh from Granny in return.

"It's early enough for the three of us to go to Crawford to the Majestic Theater and I'll get the tickets. I've heard you've never been to the movies and the matinee would keep us there until supper time. Have you ever heard of Charlie Chaplin or Al Jolson?"

She paused for a moment before speaking, "I have several things to say. First of all I am very glad Heidi will be with us. I love her almost as much as I love Gloria. You couldn't find many in this world better than her to spend time with. And I've seen Mr. Chaplin's picture in a magazine and often wondered why folks figure he's so funny although he looked funny. And one of my lady friends at church had me over for tea a while back and she played a song on her Victrola with Mr. Jolson singing and some of the words were that he'd walk a million miles for one of his mother's smiles. And I have seen magic lantern slides missionaries showed at church but I've never seen an actual movie. So this sounds like a good adventure for me. And I'll feel safe with a U.S. Marshal watching over Heidi and me."

"Granny, I want you to know that the funny man has a silent movie they will be playing first. A good musician will play either the piano or organ as the movie is shown with tunes that go along with what is happening. They are going to show a film called The Kid and some words will also show for our understanding. The second film is The Jazz Singer featuring sound and I'm quite sure the song mentioning a million miles is part of it. Heidi was very certain we would all enjoy the pictures. And afterwards I plan that we will dine at Armstrong's Café and I have heard they have an excellent reputation."

Garth was made to sit between the two ladies in the theater. Granny was very impressed by the opulence of the place. It had first been a music hall for operas and various concerts including school shows. Now it was primarily a movie house. He explained to the women that there were several theaters in Chicago with two or three times the seating and the very latest Hollywood offerings were usually featured.

All three of them had a number of good laughs along with the audience at some of the antics in the silent Chaplin film and applause was actually sustained after the Jolson film was concluded. The only negative was that Granny developed a tickle in her throat and tried to stifle any coughing. Once back in the Ford, Garth took a package of Smith Brother's cough drops out of his map box and gave them to her explaining they often soothed him after giving a lesson to school children and they worked best by just letting them melt in the mouth.

Armstrong's Café was only a few blocks from the theater and was a family-oriented restaurant. Heidi told the others she had eaten a rather late dinner and would be very content with a small tuna salad and perhaps a scoop of ice cream for dessert. Both of the others had eaten sparsely at breakfast and lunch and both wanted breaded pork chop dinners which the older woman insisted would be hard to equal at home. And they both had cherry tarts alamode.

But the events of the day and the movies almost were too much for Granny's respiration and she could tell her blood pressure was higher than was good for her. She excused the start of her coughing and wheezing as they were finishing at the table and took out her ever close medication and took two tables explaining that the doctor cautioned her on never using three in a day without checking with him.

Garth waited at the table until Granny was breathing easier and her ruddy complexion a bit paler before he paid the check and ordered the ladies to remain seated until he brought the car around to the entrance. He then asked Heidi to scoot into the rear seat of the two-door and assisted Granny in front. He handed her a small pillow for her head and a blanket for it did require a few miles of driving to warm the interior. The old woman actually dozed off within minutes of the drive home.

Heidi and Garth discussed their evening and commented about the entertaining films and pleasant atmosphere. But she also said she hoped that Granny was not going to have bad repercussions from the strenuous events of the day. "I think it would be best if I helped her get to bed. She seems fine except she would never want to admit he had perhaps over done things. And she told me in secret about what was being planned regarding the Trust. But all that was deliberately held back from Gloria. You wouldn't mind the delay bringing me home, would you?"

He answered, "I think we both feel Mrs. Miller ought not to be bothered when it would be best for her to have her evening with the kids and her hubby. And I'm not worried about my rest. It's not yet much after eight and it's a good change of pace for me to have a chance to gab with someone in my age bracket."

She said, "So when you get me home, perhaps we could sit in the restaurant which closes at eight thirty anyhow and perhaps sip some cola or ginger ale unless you'd rather have coffee and then I'd appreciate it if you could bring back a birthday gift and hide it in your room."

"That would be fine. I've already a little something for the boy I picked up at the five and dime they were putting on sale. It's a kite, actually, with a ball of string, but for the life of me I have no knowledge of putting it together or flying it. But I'm pretty sure Burly could help out there."

She agreed and when they roused Granny and got her safely in her room, the man quickly went back to the waiting room. About then Burly came up and quietly greeted the Marshal. "Marshal Stone, I just stoked up the furnace enough and opened the registers down there cuz that's where the party will be and it is a little chilly. And in the morning could you help me set up the saw horses and planks for a table for the lunch? And just so you don't worry about anything, I kin set up Mark's kite and also teach him how to fly it."

In Swede's dining room most of the lights were out so Heidi lit a table lamp and brought them both cold ginger ales. She sat down across from him in the small circle of light and they could not be seen in the corner from outside. She was silent a moment, almost as if too nervous to break the pleasant silence. She then sipped a bit of her beverage and cleared her throat. "Well?"

"Well what?"

"Well what would you like to talk about, Garth?"

"I guess I'm worried about Mrs. Miller. I don't know Frank's age, but it seems to me there are way too many years between them. She's so young and she married so early. From all I've seen and heard they're almost a perfect couple but I have silly misgivings about what might transpire in ten or twenty years."

"Garth, do you love her?"

"Uh, I admire her character. She's such a kind person. Such a faithful wife and a great example of what a mother ought to be."

"Mr. U.S. Marshal, do you love her?"

"I like her a lot. I really do."

"You're getting me annoyed. I better take a different tack. Can you tell me you love me?"

This shocked the man. "What? I feel the same way toward you as to her. You're a good person. I like you a lot."

"Do you love my folks and Granny and Mark and Maggie and every stranger you meet. And what does Jesus have to say about love? Did he ever tell you that you should just like people? Just what did He say?"

Garth was totally shocked as His Lord's words burned inside him. He looked away from the pretty young lady and his eyes fell on one of the nearby wall plaques that said God Is Love. He took a few sips to moisten his throat and then reached across the table to hold her hands gently as his eyes focused on hers. He noticed that her eyes were moist.

"Heidi, My Jesus said that God loves me and if I love God I must obey Him. He also said I was to love every other believer. And I was further told to love every neighbor and that meant as in the Good Samaritan story to turn my love into deeds. And I can also detect your distaste for the word like. But I also have to admit that there are people I have known that God expects me to love but that doesn't mean I have to like them if they keep doing evil."

She answered, "I feel the same way. I heard a preacher say God expects us to love sinners but hate the sin. And I'm sure you must have a lot of God's love in you for those around you but you're too chicken to say love instead of like."

"Touché, Heidi. But relating to Frank and Gloria, do you think their marriage was the result of love or just passion?"

"I'm sure they will gladly admit that most of the facts are public or strongly suspected. But let me tell a condensed version of the events. The three men arrived in town in the Buick in 1933 and at first stayed at Stein's boarding house where they each had separate rooms and breakfast and supper. The tale they told was that they wanted a law-abiding town to set up office for their business and would be out of town quite frequently. I believed they arrived in mid-September.

"Gloria was 14 then but strangers always considered her looks to be those of a girl in her late teens. Up till then she did any cleaning chores including dishes to earn whatever she could to help Granny to provide for her and her brother. She's about eight years older than him and they've been dependent on Granny because their parents both died before Mark was born.

"Anyhow she was so pleasant to customers that my dad hired her as a part-time waitress and those three men were always complimentary to her especially Frank and they would always give her tips. Now Prohibition was repealed on December fifth, a Tuesday, and there was going to be a celebration on Saturday evening of the ninth. By then beer and wine were available.

"Now Gloria's birthday would fall on the following Saturday so a surprise was planned for her in advance. At a signal to the guests the birthday song was sung and my mother pinned a corsage on her apron and my dad told her she was to be a part of the celebration but was forbidden to serve as a waitress, yet would receive the full pay. And then a birthday cake was brought to the table where she had been seated with the three men. There were no candles on but it was large enough for each celebrant to have a piece.

"She was the center of attention and was quite easily induced to drink some of the sweet wine. But as the evening wore on she was persuaded to take in several more small glasses. She should never have been coaxed for after a few

48

hours she began getting very dizzy. By then the folks were mostly heading home when she fainted away. It had been planned for her to stay with me that night but I also had been foolish and as the saying goes had a buzz on. She would have gone to church with us but Frank assured me he could get her home safely although he was also pretty tipsy to be driving the Buick.

"Burly and Jacob were close to drunk when they left and both felt the short walk to the boarding house would clear their heads. The Buick was there by the time they arrived. The next morning Gloria awoke with an awful hangover and she was under the covers with Frank. They both groaned and Burly brought them each aspirins.

"Gloria and Frank both swore that neither of them had any recollection of what happened. They had after all both been declared totally intoxicated. But the men knew that witnesses from the party would very likely have their own convictions about what happened and since the girl had never before been drunk and was very much under age, ancient lynch law could possibly be enacted.

"Frank quickly contacted the Sheriff and then went to Granny and confessed that he really didn't know what had happened but for several months his affection had grown and it had to be love and he with permission of Granny who was the girl's guardian and also with the permission of the possibly offended party would as soon as possible marry her if there was any possibility she could accept him but he really preferred a non-church wedding performed by a Justice of the Peace. There was a rapid agreement by all parties and the two were wed on Wednesday in Crawford with Burly and Jacob as witnesses and signed documents attesting to the union.

"They had no honeymoon but Frank immediately leased an apartment from Gloria's grandmother and also a double room upstairs for the other two men. It was not fully known the bride was pregnant until about a month after the wedding and Margaret was born on the 30th of August in 1934. So that's the basic story and Gloria and Granny have had nothing but praise for the treatment all of them have seen and received. Perhaps all is well that ends well.

"Oh! One more thing I have to mention. Both of them before they got their license had complete health checks which included blood tests lest there could have been any disease which could have endangered either of them. But had there been anything bad, I don't think the license would have been allowed. But other things such as alcohol were never mentioned."

The pair had a brief discussion in which both agreed that God is love and He is the source of true love and that liking others was really an aspect of love but that what too many called love ought correctly be named lust and a desire for people to get what they want and not give what was properly needed. They both felt that the other had deep inner convictions as to what was pleasing to God.

Just before the man left she handed him the gift-wrapped package tagged for the birthday boy. "Garth, would you please stash this in your room until after the party's over and the children go home? We know that most of them come from families with very limited means and we don't want them to feel bad that their gifts might be very limited. My folks and a few of the regular customers who know Gloria have chipped in and designated me to go to the New and Used Book Store and get some used books for Mark. With Gloria and Granny helping he has done a remarkable job of learning to read in his first three grades. I got Pinocchio, Tom Sawyer, Huckleberry Finn, and The Riders of the Purple Sage plus a small Dictionary. I'm sure he'll be delighted."

Garth went to bed that night with very pleasant memories of the busy day and his thoughts did keep going to the young mother, but he also realized that Heidi had depths of thought he really appreciated. He was very glad he had met her and rejoiced that he could genuinely consider her as a good friend.

Burly and Garth quickly got the plank tables set up Saturday morning. They also hung up streamers and little decorations in the basement. Jacob and Frank did a change of pace and amused Maggie and Maureen after breakfast and also included the birthday boy. This freed Gloria and Dharma to help Granny in the kitchen as the older woman baked and decorated a large three layer birthday cake.

The other women prepared big pitchers of Kool-Aid and platters of sandwiches. Chicken, tuna salad, and perennially favorite peanut butter and jelly were cut into traditional triangles small mouths could easily attack. The party had been planned to serve lunch first. This was followed by the Happy Birthday song as the cake with ten lighted candles was set before Mark. He blew them all out and absolutely refused to even hint what he had wished for. And all celebrants were given generous pieces of cake with a small scoop of ice cream.

Before the dozen or so children began arriving the lad had privately opened what his daddy and two uncles had brought him as well as a totally unexpected gift from Garth. He had from Granny and Gloria been given underwear and sox. He had ever since his sister's marriage been calling the couple mama and daddy. The man had somewhere procured a beautiful shiny brass telescope in a leather tube with a sturdy neck strap. He was amazed at how it pulled out to give an image four or five times larger than what the lad's unaided eye could see.

That morning as the party room was being prepared, Burly explained about the uncle title. "Garth, I been helpin' Frank for about four years now. And Jacob and him and me were all orphans. And we got along so well it seemed almost like we was family and we used to joke about bein' the three musketeers. It felt just like we were actually brothers. And when Gloria was one of us it was like we were brothers-in-law to her. So naturally we were uncles. And I think she'd like it if you were added to her kids' uncles like Clancy." It became a done deal.

Uncle Burly's gift was a military design compass with folding sights to more easily get a bearing. It had a khaki canvas case and also had a neck strap. The lad was intrigued that even if it was pitch-black out, the needle and dial glowed. He was also shown how bringing it near iron would affect the needle.

Then Uncle Jacob gave him another piece of soldier equipment, a canteen with a khaki case. This had a clip which could secure it to a military or civilian belt. He was told that in hot weather it kept the water cool longer if the cover was wet.

Gloria told Mark his father thought it would be okay if he called the Marshal Uncle. And though the gift was the very least cost wise he treasured it equally for he had often seen bigger kids flying such things but none of them had a telescope to make theirs look close. All told, he felt like a rich kid. But he was well trained by his sister-mother to always be thankful and never belittle a gift no matter how inexpensive it was or if it might be second-hand.

The boy received some purchased cards and many which had been printed by his friends. He got a used soft rubber ball which could bounce up to the ceiling if thrown down hard. He also got a used yo-yo and a top with a string to wind it to propel it. He got a rather shrill whistle and then from the ones with the least available came coins, mostly pennies, in the cards. In Mark's space was an old wooden cigar box which was had been painted and trimmed so he thought of it as his treasure chest and with previous coins and his new additions made him feel very wealthy.

The noise from the crowd of often boisterous children was almost too much for Frank to endure and once the basement activities were nearly over, he went upstairs to the waiting room to the reclining chair and also took a little bit of tonic. He was a bit surprised that Jacob who usually was not very communicative with youngsters and usually had a very serious expression spent time below asking riddles and telling a few humorous accounts from his own childhood.

Burly had always been cheerful and full of encouraging words. And he went before the children holding a red-nosed clown mask with a curly blue wig. He had said, "Some little kids are afraid of clowns and so I wanted all of you to see me put this silly thing on and my clown name is Dum-dum.

All of you should sit down on the gym mats and I wanna show you some tricks. See these little rubber balloons? I kin puff 'em up and make little dogs and stuff for each of you."

While the small mob was seated, Garth passed around bowls of fresh popcorn and peanuts in the shell. Dum-dum said in a very squeaky voice. "You better not leave any shells on the floor when you're done or the peanut shell police will arrest you."

After a game of Pin the Tail on the Donkey and a few other simple diversions, Granny called down the stairs, "Children, if the shells are all in the waste basket, and the critters that Dum-dum made for you aren't popped yet, leave them all on the table. You need to come up and go into the front yard inside the picket fence. There's a special treat coming for every one of you."

By the time the gang was lined up inside the fence, Gene Rogers, his son, and a stable boy were there with three ponies to give every child a good ride north to the corner and then east past Good Shepherd Lutheran and then back to Granny's. The streets in Stillwell formed a big checkerboard with quarter mile intervals in each direction allowing all residents to have large back areas great for gardening and playing. Rogers Livery, an old landmark, was about halfway to the next street south.

Each child including Maggie and Maureen had great safe rides on the gentle beasts which had been used for frequent municipal affairs meant to excite children. But in addition to those who guided the ponies, Gloria's husband and his partners made sure each and every child was steadied and reassured. When all the rides were completed, everyone was told to be sure to thank the Sheriff and his department for they had paid for this adventure. And as the children departed with their animal-like balloons (Dum-dum replaced those which had burst) Dharma and Clancy herded them back to the church playground to await the pickup by parents.

Burly assembled Mark's kite and took him and Jacob to the High School football field a few blocks away for a glorious time of launching and flying the kite with even the Treasurer running like a child for launch power. Frank by then was very uncomfortable and chose to nap a bit. But the telescope he had given made viewing the little flyer a delight also. And the boy could hardly believe it when after supper he saw his books. He said, "And all I wished for was a chance to ride a horse."

There was one discordant note to Gloria's day. Too many things that day had been out of his control and Frank was crabby and critical. Before their supper he took her aside and gave her a controlled tongue-lashing without first asking why something was done or giving her a chance to explain. This was so unlike him that the woman had a hard time holding back tears.

"From our window I saw you taking a walk with the Marshal and you held his arm. He was carrying Maggie on his shoulders and she's my daughter and doesn't need you to have a handsome young man tending to her. When we're away I don't go out with unmarried women or widows unless some of her older relatives or Burly or Jacob are along. You know your Bible says to avoid the very appearance of evil. I do everything I can to prevent gossipers and snoops from giving away bad reports about me. And I expect the same from you. I expect to be the only important man in your life. Do you understand? Can you assure me there will never be a bad report about you?"

By now there were tears running down her face for her tender heart would never allow her to harm her husband but she had done no wrong. She threw her arms around him and tried to kiss him but he turned his face away and pushed her away. "Sweetheart, if I hurt you I didn't do anything bad or on purpose. Please let me tell you. I'm sorry if I hurt you any way."

In return he faced her and looked distressed. "I guess I spoke too soon and too sharp. It's these blasted headaches. I guess I'm sorry I'm so gruff sometimes. But I love you so much, I feel hurt too much sometimes. Okay. Tell me your side."

She hugged him again and he returned it gently and softly returned her kiss. "Thank you dear. And you don't need to be sorry. It was like this. Mark and Burly and Jacob were going ahead to the football field and we were going to meet them there but first take Maggie to the playground and push her on the swing. The little dear was already getting pretty tired and she held out her arms for her new Uncle Garth to carry her. So he put her up on his shoulders and steadied her with his right arm behind her back.

"But about then a piece of gravel slid into my right shoe and I grabbed his left arm to steady myself so I could slip the shoe off and empty it. I remember that a big truck went by about that time and you couldn't have seen me for a few seconds. And then the playground is out of sight and she squealed on the swing ride. And then we joined the others and sat on the bleachers to watch our three brave pilots fly a paper aircraft. And we all came home together."

He quite gently moved her over to the sofa and sat down close to her with his arm around her and she rested her head on his shoulder and to her once again all was well with the world. She never consciously considered it but she felt that she would always be the best possible wife to him and would never dare to displease him.

He cleared his throat and in his customary smooth and soft words said, "I really am sorry. And regarding young men who are our friends and offer to escort you or help you by giving you a ride when needed, well I will trust them if you and Granny or the Uncles do. And since Burly is just like an older brother to you, and a good driver, the things I've just mentioned could never have an appearance of evil to them."

Garth took Heidi out for a sundae that evening and he related the happenings at the birthday party she had not been able to take part in due to things that needed to be attended to at Swede's Place. He made it a point to list names of all the people in town he loved since their previous talk about liking folks. She got the point and threw back at him what seemed like an endless list until they both laughed and called their word war time for an Armistice.

But it also seemed to both of them before sleep came that knowing in your heart that God shows others His love through you is what counts. Garth had vivid images after a time of prayer of those such as Gloria and her family and also Heidi and her family.

CHAPTER THREE

Mark's birthday seemed to him to have been the very best day he could remember. He could hardly believe so many people including adults would ever have done so many nice things to and for him. And all his young friends had raved about Dum-dum and the games and pony rides and cake etc. It had tuckered him and his sister out so much neither of them tried to avoid bedtime.

Granny was also worn out by the time the party was over. Friday's meeting to set up a combined Brown and Miller Trust and then the much approved plan to build and start Gloria's Shoppe had taken a great weight off the mind of Hester Sue for she was now sure her granddaughter would be well provided for no matter what transpired, even if God allowed the young lady to lose her grandma.

Going to her very first movies and eating out at Armstrong's had also drained her strength and brought on unavoidable throat and respiratory difficulty and she had been aware of her pulse and blood pressure increasing. She knew she should have done only a fraction of Mark's birthday lunch and cake work. She could have accepted more help but it had to be just so for the sweet boy. That afternoon she knew she ought to take in some light nourishment and rest as much as possible but like so many women she always seemed to have just one more little thing she really had to do first.

She ended up in bed and added her lap quilt to her usual covers. She had alternate chills and hot flashes and was having trouble getting deep breaths beside which her throat was sore and hurt each time she coughed. She silently communed with God to thank him for all the good things including her own gratitude that Gloria would be well provided for no matter what came. And she was especially grateful for Burly whose faith and actions were so much like her handsome Harry and their son Gerald.

Burly had ever been willing to fulfill needed tasks. Shortly after moving in, when free time permitted, he had done a beautiful job of painting the long picket fence around the house. The following year a violent windstorm had knocked tree limbs against the roof and he had done needful re-shingling. Besides numerous little fix-it jobs he had also run a wire from her bed table through the basement to Gloria's apartment door bell. Granny had at first thought it to be unnecessary but as her health left her with more and more difficulties, it seemed a good idea that she could easily ring for help if it became necessary.

Granny glanced at the alarm clock on the dresser. She was shocked that she was so very exhausted but it was only six and a terrible headache was coming on to add to her raw throat. She really wished she didn't have to call Gloria but she was unable to think clearly and she began to push the button to ask for aid.

The Millers had just finished supper, mostly leftovers from the birthday lunch and cake. Frank said to his wife,

"You better rush to see what's wrong. Since the kids are already in their night clothes, I'll see if one of the O'Connors can see to getting them to bed and I'll be with you in a jiffy."

It did take a few minutes before Dharma could come over, and when Frank arrived by Granny's bedside, he immediately used the office phone to urge Dr. Williams to do a quick check on the elderly woman. After just a few minutes the Dr. was there with his bag and did a quick check on blood pressure and used his stethoscope to check her breathing and examined her throat and temperature. It's amazing how much physicians can accomplish in such a short time. He ascertained that the lady's general health was less good than his last visit to her but reassured the Millers that simple remedies could do a great deal for her.

"She needs fluids. An easy help will be hot herb tea with lots of lemon and honey in it. Then she ought to have hot chicken broth and I have a couple of packets of powder to mix in the soup. These will act to calm her and make her very drowsy and also ease her headache. There is also a lowering effect for her blood pressure. Remember she needs lots of hot fluids.

"I also have some salve which is much like liniment with menthol which she should have on her upper back and chest and on her neck and keep her warm. My helper Nurse Hillman borrowed my car to run a couple of errands and she should be back in maybe fifteen minutes and I know Ruth will be glad to check on Granny every few hours.

"Then in the morning this feisty old gal will be needing good nourishment but nothing hard to swallow or digest. And poached eggs and apple sauce and maybe some Jell-O along with more special tea would be good. Later on avoid too much spice or hard to chew items. I'll leave some of the powders to use as needed. Just remember she mostly needs rest and fluids and nourishment.

"Tomorrow I insist she have a very tranquil day of rest. I don't think she should go to church but I know there are a couple of services on the radio. And until church is over, I'm sure Ruth will be glad to take care of her."

After dinner Jacob requested Burly and Garth to investigate the possible purchase of a second vehicle for Miller Associates. A newspaper ad had offered a Buick sedan identical to the car to which Burly held the title. The business had to have a car but had been behind in salary to the big man and to compensate had signed it over to him.

A couple of blocks away there was the Pulaski Barber Shop on the corner with entrances on both streets. Just south of it was the Pulaski home. The car owner, Erica Pulaski, was recently widowed. Her eldest son was now in charge and she, a good beautician, still had a goodly number of ladies who also visited her at the shop. She knew Granny and Gloria and was very friendly to the men who first phoned before stopping by.

Jacob explained before the trio went to see the widow or her car. "Burly has been a terrific help to our business. But we can never expand and get branch offices with just one car. There are at least six promising locations within a couple of hundred miles. But we need to be sure the people who become involved with us meet our qualifications. And for this we need to be able to see them face to face on a regular basis. Letters and phone calls help but direct contact is a matter of necessity. And Burly is a great driver and upkeep and repair man but he owns his car and we could not in good conscience let him wear it out. And if we think it through, we can see the advantage of a car that belongs to Miller Associates.

"Garth, I'm sure you're wondering why we asked you along. Well, if I make Mrs. Pulaski an offer, you are a third party witness, as to what I say so there is no question about it later. Some times an old person's memory is shaky until papers are signed and I would never want anyone to think there was any shadiness to what was done. I would never try to defraud anyone. You were at the trust meeting and I am absolutely certain that no one there thought there was even a hint of illegality or possible depriving of Mrs. Miller as to what she should get."

Mrs. Pulaski quickly led the trio to the garage behind the home to show them the auto she wished to sell. After Burly did a quick check of tires, oil, and a few other essentials, he started the machine which was a twin to his. A grandson of the widow had been diligent in washing and waxing the sparkling car and between times used a charger to maintain the battery. The old lady refused to go along for a short drive for the only times she had rode in it was when she and her husband had taken vacation trips or ran errands together. Her memories gave her too much pain and since she was a very petite woman it was beyond her desire or strength to ever drive it.

When the men returned with nothing but good to say about the sturdy automobile Erica told a bit about it. "My husband Basil bought it about the same time Gloria got married. It was used but only had a couple of thousand miles on it. We had both spent so many years with barbering and beauty work that we never had a real vacation. But by then my oldest boy was already a great barber and his wife could do permanents. So during the next three summers we travelled. We went to Chicago and visited the Zoo and a couple of museums and even went swimming at Montrose Beach. Another trip was to Gettysburg and the Hershey Chocolate Factory. Our last trip was to Niagara Falls. And we bought dozens of post cards and took dozens of pictures. If you have time someday, I'd be glad to show you our albums."

Burly assured the woman that her machine was worth every penny she was asking for it since mechanically everything worked as it should. Garth admitted he did not have any good knowledge of value of used cars but that the price did seem very fair and the woman could have asked more and allowed herself to be dickered down the way used car dealers often did.

Then Jacob showed her a number of possible financial arrangements that could be safely and fairly be used. "Madam, your price couldn't be better. But at the moment Miller Associates is involved in several possible extensions of our business by starting some branch offices and I will need to travel within a few days to see about getting branch offices started. We very much wish to avoid having to deal with financial institutions but our funds are limited. However I also believe there is a safe and good alternate available.

"The very most cash I can deliver to you immediately is about 10% of your fair asking price. But it might take as much as 30 days to pay you more. And that does not help your immediate plans even with a fair interest rate. But I do need to use a safe strong machine as soon as possible. Burly has said I could borrow his but it is needed here and it is only proper that he not be hampered in his possible transportation needs.

"So it has occurred to us that perhaps I could rent your machine and that 10% could cover the mileage costs of using it. Then when the 30 days expire, you would still be the owner and could still sell it. It is to be understood that when we rent a car, all repairs, maintenance, and excess mileage costs are our responsibility. But if fortune smiles on us and we can then pay the balance, we all come out ahead. Also since I would have my copy of the rental agreement with me there could never be any legal question about my right to use it. I also must say I would like to give you a bigger percentage at the start, but then I wouldn't have the cash I need for lodging and meals as I travel. And your title to the car is not encumbered."

Erica asked the Marshal what he thought of it all. He replied, "I can't give legal advice but from what I've seen and heard, I think this would be a good and safe deal. I know nothing about mileage cost but what Jacob showed you came right from car dealer quotes. And judging by how Granny and Gloria and the kids have been treated by these business men, it looks like you're being offered a fair and safe deal. They certainly seem like good business men whose deals are the kind that won't hurt anyone."

Mrs. Pulaski agreed with the Marshal but she also had never made any substantial deals without first conferring with her husband and since he was now in Heaven she always took advice from her son, Alfred, who was the head of their barber business. He lived in the upper floor above the shop with his wife, Ursa, and the teenaged boy and girl grandchildren of Erica. They were just arriving home from a friend's house where they'd gone for dinner. Alfred hurried over to Mom's house as she was showing the trio some of her trip photos.

After a good presentation by Jacob and encouraging words from Garth, he agreed with his mother that it made sense and looked like a good thing to do. He had said, "Mom, you know that our Chevy runs great and we would always be able to give you a lift. Plus my son will be graduating from High School next June and he has been saving up to get a pickup truck. He loves to haul things and he would also be as proud as a peacock if you let him taxi you around. And we know you don't want to learn to drive and also it's tough to have so many memories. So do it, Mom. Add some more cash to your buried treasure. Or have you actually been socking away loot in the bank?"

Erica grinned back at Alfred over what had apparently been a family joke. "Al, you know better than that. I still keep it hid under my mattress and my 12 gage still sets beside my night table." And then she laughed as did the others. "So let's sign the papers and I want my son and Garth to undersign my name"

Jacob said, "I want our agreed cash to go from my hand to yours first." His rather bulky wallet had a chain fastened to his belt and he ostentatiously opened it and counted out the currency. "Okay. First a receipt, then the rental papers, and then also the third paper which is our agreement to the change of title after all is paid. Does that seem okay?"

The transaction was completed by mid-afternoon. Garth rode back to Granny's with Burly and the Miller family all had a short jaunt with Jacob driving to show off the new "company car." Garth was sure it was a good move for all concerned and he wished to share the news with Heidi. It was an acceptable reason to spend some pleasant moments chatting with the light blond lady. But he also thought of how she'd mentioned to him about how all her life she'd enjoyed horse-back riding.

So he'd given an invitation to her to go for a ride with him. Within a half an hour he had picked her up to drive her to Roger's Livery to get a couple of horses for a pleasant ride past the depot and then north across the Pine River a while before turning back. She deliberately embarrassed him by mentioning to him the good things Gloria, Granny, and her mom and dad had said about him. "Garth, I am positively amazed at how many paths of good people God has allowed to cross my path and that I can say I'm glad to have as friends."

He replied, "I feel the same way. And I can't tell you how each person I get to know adds ideas and encouragement to me. And you have a good idea of the direction my life is headed, but I really don't know much about you. Tell me your plans for the future, if you will, and perhaps, if I'm not too bold, about your ideas. I have noticed that you don't have an engagement ring and if you had been wearing one I would not have sought to get to know you better. It wouldn't be proper."

"In other words you try to be very careful not to infringe on some fellow's territory. Well, I know a load of guys and gals but at the moment I am not yet spoken for. However there are a few fellows Gloria has said might be good prospects. The truth of the matter is that I am beginning to believe that God is pointing me in the direction of working with children and when the right man comes along for a life-long commitment; Jesus will make it crystal clear to me.

"Gloria and I are almost the same age but she left school when she got married and I went on to get my 12th grade diploma. And she has excellent reading and math skills. After my graduation I took a few night classes at Crawford Community College. Many subjects are offered to those who have day jobs but can spare one or two evenings. I sort of have a day job at the restaurant but a fellow grad has been going two nights a week and I get a free ride in the pickup truck. He's Herbert Wilson whose dad owns the Wilson Hardware and doesn't need the truck in the evenings."

Garth asked, "Is this fellow someone you and your folks trust?"

"Oh yes. I've known Herbie since 4th grade. And the Wilsons are all staunch Baptists. But he's quite bashful around strangers unless they're youngsters. He wants to be a grade school teacher and that's the age of kids I love the most. I have mixed emotions right now about whether I want to become a Licensed Practical Nurse or a teacher like Herbie. So right now one of my night classes is about first aid and the other is an introduction to pedagogy. I think I could be happy about teaching or child care in an orphanage or such place. But I'd be happiest if God sent Mr. Right my way so I could be free from moving from place to place."

"Heidi, what if God wants you to be the spouse of a missionary who might have to be changing address quite often to meet the needs of others, both adults and children? Or a soldier, or fireman, or policeman? Could you be content to be half of a team of people who need to frequently move to meet other needs in other places? For example I never dreamed I'd become a government employee who might have to make changes. I haven't tried to plan ahead but when Major Colfax informed me I'd be back for a few weeks to the hometown of my early childhood, I welcomed the chance of using my skills and training to aid law officers, rangers, sportsmen, and even high school kids. God does move in mysterious ways and he does allow folks to cross my paths and brighten lonesome hours."

About this time their rides and rambling chats ceased at Roger's Livery as they returned the horses. She did not just then wish to continue in the vein of thought in which they had been dwelling. She asked, "What have you eaten today? Did you have a good breakfast? Or just coffee and a pastry?"

He admitted it was a good guess and she immediately asked about his Sunday dinner. He told her he'd heated a can of soup on his hot plate and she said, "I feel sorry for you. A growing child like you needs more than that. You will obey me and enter the restaurant with me and I will order you to eat my atrocious cooking until you're stuffed. And when my mother knows what's going on there's an excellent chance she might help me and even reveal some of her culinary secrets to me."

The two of them were actually ordered by the mother to use the private dining room and both her parents served them a banquet of heated leftovers from dinner with plenty of coffee. Heidi told the man, "This was not planned and I never expected such a thing. But parents seem to have a better idea about things than they let on. It's nicer this way because I have some things I'd like to learn from you."

She asked the blessing this time and they ate slowly so they could talk. She asked him to tell her enough of his background so she wouldn't be wondering about this man of mystery and particularly about his ability with horses and his obvious affection and kindness for them.

He responded, "It's still pretty early so if you don't mind I'll get to the best part of that story which involves Jesse James and Belle Star. But I'll need to add a bit of geography so you may take a nap while I'm gabbing. Of course you can sip some more coffee to stay awake during my National Geographic lecture."

"Stick to the main details, Cowboy. I studied geography in High School."

"Okay. You know that the Pine River which runs along the north end of town flows about 40 miles until it joins the Eagle River as it flows south from Canada. And Eagle Island which is about 12 miles long and a mile and a half at its widest divides the Eagle River. The Island remained state territory after statehood and had no permanent homes on it until several years after the first wagon train settled here. Our state wanted more residents, particularly farmers and dairymen so very low purchase prices were offered to settlers.

"I am sure you have heard about Amish folks in Pennsylvania and Indiana. These are godly Christians but they have chosen to continue with old-fashioned ideas about cars and electricity and telephones and even public schools. And most of them have rural lives but many are very well skilled carpenters and it is hard to find better built furniture than they can produce. So a number of Amish families totaling perhaps 60 people migrated to Eagle Island.

"I ought to mention that when the railroad came through it crossed the center of the Island and in more recent years a highway was put through alongside the tracks. There is also a more recent covered bridge at the south end. And most of the southern end has a great deal of quite flat land very well suited for gardens and farms and pastures. The northern half of the island is hillier and more heavily forested and excellent for hunting. And now a question for you; have you heard of the Stone House and how it got its name?"

"Mr. Smarty-pants, I haven't got a clue."

"I guess you ain't Miss Know-it-all. When the Amish families arrived they immediately started gardens and prepared for plowing but some Professors are sure there had been an Ice Age and the slow-moving glaciers carried rocks along so these hard-working folks had to begin clearing the way for planting and they used the stones to make a foundation for a barn. Inside the barn they took dirt out and did what some builders call earth berming to cover the lower half of the foundation thus keeping it warmer for livestock in winter. Later after conventional sheds and barns were erected they abandoned their log shelters and added a second story which became a dormitory for the folks until additional houses could be built."

Heidi asked, "Are you ever going to get to the part about the outlaws?"

"All in due time. But first I must be sure you understand about the Stone House. After a few decades Amish began selling their property and moving back to their clans. Much of their land was sold to new immigrants. The majority of the newcomers were American Indians many of whom were married to non-Indians. There were a few Negroes, some Hispanics, and several small families of my kinfolks.

The Stones together bought the former stone foundation home used by the Amish. But this purchase was actually a lease with yearly payments. Also since many of the Amish were very well skilled craftsmen, much of the furniture and cupboards had been made by them."

Heidi sighed with obviously faked annoyance and interrupted saying, "Do all Federal Marshals go around in circles? What about the outlaws?"

"I'll get there. And all lawmen get mixed up when in the presence of a pretty blond lady. I have to first tell about how the Amish raise and use horses for farm work and they don't like to use fancy horses. In particular the Indians do seem to like horses with several colors which some call paints. But the Amish sold horses they raised when they moved except for some needed to pull their wagons back to their home states. However the Stones who still live on Eagle Island did buy a couple of paints which were not Amish owned. And I will tell you now that the Stone House has the family name of Stone along with the descriptive word of stone used as a foundation. Do you understand the term Stone House now?"

"Yes, I do. But I'll ask again, Garth. What about the outlaws?"

"Okay, I'll explain it all. First of all I have cousins, second or third that live in the Stone House. The relationship is a bit obscure. But as is our custom they are Uncle Rudolph and Aunt Elizabeth to me. But it's Rudy and Liz. They purchased a closed wagon from the Amish but the horses came from one of Chief Tootoosee's relatives. The mare and stallion were parents of two youngsters, sister and brother about a year apart. But both had very similar coloring and marking.

In particular were dark brown streaks across the lighter tan background on their faces. Some of the children who later saw them together thought they looked like outlaws they'd read about so they were named Belle Starr and Jesse James.

"But no two outlaws could have been gentler or more cooperative. Jesse was gelded for too often stallions could be less than gentle or easy to get along with. But the elder sister and younger brother got along perfectly and were quick to become friendly to any who worked them. It also seemed that they preferred each other's company more than the other horses. They loved to be ridden and loved to pull a wagon together. But Chief Tootoosee who is now the Mayor of what was named Ottawa Village admitted that they did not particularly like pulling plows."

Heidi asked as he paused to sip more coffee, "You really haven't said anything about how you learned to ride and shoot so well. And I'm much more interested about what led you to your career. Almost nothing is known about your childhood. Or is it something you'd rather not talk about?"

He paused a bit to consider whether he would and then said, "I'll give you a brief summary. My father Garrison was considerably older than my mother Jessica when they married but she was in her twenties. He always said he'd never seen a prettier gal. She was very petite and graceful but the family later on learned that her health was not equal to the tough farm life and harsh winters. After a few years my brother Gordon was born and he joined the Army as soon as he was of age but he died in the trenches of Europe when I was just a little guy. In early March after Gordon's death the cold and damp killed my mother. My dad was told Consumption killed her.

"Our farm had way too many bills coming in and overdue taxes and late mortgage payments and without money for extra help and all his grief my dad managed to sell everything and get a sturdy truck and we moved to a farm an uncle had near St. Ignace. My dad was a tremendous fisherman and hunter and the land in the U.P. of Michigan is much like here and one thing led to another and soon my dad was getting jobs as a guide for well-to-do big city sportsmen and I always went along.

"Soon the word got around and he got offers to guide groups in the mountains of Montana to go after big game and mountain goats. These trips were always done on horseback with pack animals. And I grew up learning all the skills of roughing it and shooting and fishing. But my dad always carried along school books and each day I had to spend time studying under his supervision.

"We ended up living north of Chicago where we lived with one of my dad's cousins who owned a farm supply store and Dad worked for him until old age wore him out. But I did get my High School Diploma and going to my graduation was the last time he was up and around for before he died. And while we lived there I got into an organization of patriots who loved to shoot and wanted to be like the Minutemen should our country need them. We went to many shooting matches and since I happened to be the best shooter after all my years of gun use and training, I seemed to always win the most trophies.

"I ended up as a Chicago Policeman and was soon assigned to assist government agents during the days of prohibition. We were out to get rum-runners and bootleggers. They were mostly allied with Chicago mobs. I happened to be the best rifleman available and I would be stationed in high spots to prevent gangsters with tommy guns from killing cops or feds during raids. I was responsible for at least eight being prevented from hurting or killing the good guys." At this point Garth ceased speaking.

Heidi noticed that the man seemed to be staring off into space. She hoped her curiosity had not invoked bad memories. She had a few times before noticed a similar reaction from soldiers who had been relating a small portion of what must have been bad memories of combat situations and probable casualties or deaths. "I'm sorry if I caused you to remember things you'd rather forget. Why don't you skip to happier things?"

"No! God gives us memory so we will learn even from the rough experiences. I've known cops who were ruined due to situations where either in self-defense or to prevent injury to innocent by-standers a law-breaker had to be shot down or even killed. The officer would never be the same again. I thank God none of the eight I shot died due to my shooting. I had the ability to take any of their lives. Only one died months later. He fled and his wound was untreated and unreported and gangrene took his life. If he had surrendered and not escaped it is almost a certainty he would have lived.

"I want to tell you a little more but I'll not describe the gore. I have killed game for food most of my early life. My father insisted we shoot to make quick kills and never allow game to suffer. When I fired at those lawbreakers and it was obvious they would kill any of us, I destroyed their ability to handle a weapon. The bullets I used in my rifle had pointed hard tips that would go through a hand or elbow or shoulder and eliminate their ability to even hold a weapon. The man who died had already wounded a fed and a cop and I hit him in the knee as he got into a getaway car. I never killed a human being; gangrene infection is what killed him. And several of the eight learned skills and after jail time did find honest jobs for partially disabled men. I don't know how many got religion but there were at least two who now claim to trust Jesus."

She was silent but reached across the table and clasped his hands and briefly squeezed them. He continued but noticed her eyes were misty. "Dear Lady, for now I would hope you'd not mention the shooting. My name was never used in any public record and the Police Commissioner preferred the Federal Agents get the credit so none of the cops would be targeted by the rulers of the mobs. Anyhow, it was after this I was offered the job of Marshal."

He sipped a bit of coffee and then said, "We remember a great deal of our past but that is History. More importantly we look to what the future holds and that is Hope. Some speak of their dreams and wishes which may define their Hope. The major areas of Hope for most people involve marriage and family plus occupational goals. Heidi, you've mentioned your dream of working with youngsters. But what about the marriage and family side? I think you have good basic wisdom but so far no specific choice in mind. Or have you begun making a list of prospects?"

There was a trace of rebellion on her face as she replied, "What about you? You're the one who has travelled far beyond my boundaries and undoubtedly could have prepared a very long list of prospects. And I'm sure your catalog of women that fit within your proper ideas of faith and grace and beauty and proper feminine abilities could be a long list." And at this point she turned away from him and had to stifle a laugh and he knew she had been putting him on.

He forced himself to wear his sternest face and with a gravelly voice such as he would use when dealing with miscreants said, "Do you realize how bad it is to refuse to cooperate with a Federal Officer of the Law? I demand to know if I am on your list." And he also fought to avoid chuckling. "I'm sorry. Forget about lists. Neither of us are adolescents."

"Mr. Marshal, I'm still just a kid and I'm scared silly of you. I'll check my list." At this she twisted around so he couldn't see her face and held up an imaginary list and ran her finger down it and murmured to herself, "Nope, he ain't there. I can't see why any girl could have an interest in him."

Garth said, "I think it would be best for us to change our direction to more serious matters. If God wrote a list, that would be the only one that mattered. If He has plans for each of us, they're the only plans that are really worthwhile. If He is leading either of us in a specific direction, that's the only one we should follow and make His plans our hopes and dreams. Heidi, do you have a specific passage of Scripture that God has been more and more implanting into you?"

"I do indeed. Ever since I was a little girl in Sunday school the teacher told all of us how Jesus had a special love for children. He told his followers to suffer the little children to come to him and never forbid them because they were part of God's kingdom. And the teacher told us that suffer was an old-fashioned word which meant to invite and persuade. And as a little girl I knew Jesus loved me and was inviting me and I became one of his lambs. And ever since I wanted to be like that teacher but more importantly I wanted to be a follower who would do whatever I could to walk in Jesus' footsteps to help and win children to him."

Garth asked, "But does that hope preclude being the wife of a man with a similar persuasion even if it means a frequent change of address?"

"I admit my plan meant being in one place so I could continue a long term work. But I've begun to see God might ask me to marry a man such as an evangelist who is ever on the move. Or perhaps a military man or some other who would be under orders to go to definite changes of address. If it was my plan it would mean a more or less permanent address. But I trust my Shepherd and I know whatever he planned would be the best plan.

"And as an aside, I'm pretty certain sure Mary and Joseph had other children and I'm absolutely sure Jesus as a youngster played with them and taught them the way older kids play and guard the rest. I'm absolutely certain that wherever Jesus went the children flocked around him. And if I do marry and have children, I'll want them to flock around him and trust him. And after seeing how well Maggie and Mark love to be around you, I'm sure you have the same kind of heart as I do. Now tell me what your life verses are."

"Heidi, way before I could read my father made me recite certain words from the Bible. And every Sunday no matter where we were we had to set aside some time to pray and sing and open up the Bible. Trust in the Lord with all thine heart; and lean not unto thine own understanding. In all thy ways acknowledge him, and he shall direct thy paths.

Those are powerful words and they are a promise from God which never fails. But the path does get dangerous and then I remember that I can do all things through Christ which strengtheneth me. And as for a list of prospective brides, all I have is a mental list of quite a few followers of Jesus I wouldn't say no to if God said to me that one of them was meant for me. And I'll admit your name might possibly have a chance to get on that list."

She replied, "Looking at it that way, your name does have a slim possibility to getting onto my list." And then she laughed and he joined her. She continued, "We will both be very wise and leave the final decision to the One who already knows the end and the beginning."

"Look at the clock, I must get going. Thank you and your folks for a great meal and I'm so glad we both call God our Father because that means we're in the very same family and since I'm the taller one I'm gonna call you my little sister."

They walked side by side to the entrance and bumped shoulders as they stopped. He reached around her to steady her and briefly gave her a squeeze which was almost a hug. She quietly said, "Good night, big brother. Say a prayer for me so I'll never forget to do what Jesus wants."

"Good night little sister and do the same for me."

When their respective bedtimes came neither had any trouble remembering the other in prayer and wondered just what God might have in mind for them. They both were aware of a pleasant attraction to the other and found it hard to fix their thoughts on more essential matters. But in neither case were there specific plans as to how to increase their fellowship. And both of them were well aware that in a few short weeks the Marshal was due for some other assignment. It makes it very difficult for two young people to plan to extend their friendships when there is very little chance to even consider long-range plans or even hopes.

After breakfast in the Miller apartment which extended to Jacob and Burly, the three men went up to meet in the double room upstairs. Burly was told there was some necessary business planning to do and his input would be welcome. As Frank and Jacob had expected the third man begged off of what to him was often over his head or his desire to delve in confusing legal matters etc.

"Hey, guys, I got some things I promised Granny I'd do. It's gettin' colder and a few of the storm windows need fixin' and I was gonna hang 'em and if you got any errands I need to run you can just give me a list. I'm also gonna check how quick we need coal. And there might be some little fixit stuff in the apartments like drippin' faucets and such. I'd like to get all caught up on the little stuff before our next trip."

Both Frank and Jacob complimented him on his conscientiousness and reminded him how much they appreciated their reduced rental prices since he had been pitching in. They assured him they would tell him anything he needed to know about future activities. In truth they had always been quite tight-lipped about many of their plans and like the military would insist on secrecy lest competitors would be able to interfere or duplicate Miller Associates' private doings. But after Burly left the room Jacob bolted the door. Right next to the door was a shelf on which was a small radio and Frank tuned in to a local station but played it softly as a convenient shield against inadvertent eavesdropping.

"Jacob, Chief Peter and I discussed this at length and I think he's right. He is renaming his product to Herbal Tonic and he is going to double the potency but the price will only be a bit more than double. And the overall cost less than two bottles of the original for only half as many bottles will be needed and the freight cost will be half. He is also introducing High Energy Tonic with triple the alertness and energy but without the sleep aids and athletes would greatly benefit for their sport activities but it would cost triple. Imagine what this could mean for sportsmen who so quickly get tired out.

"Now the markup for the salesmen totals 25%. But if we became Chief Peter's go-betweens and handled all the paper we would allow our agents to keep 20% and do all the work of selling. But all purchases for our agents have to go through us. I'm not as good with the math as you Jacob but if we can set up a network and a hundred cases a month go through it, our puny cut grows to about twice what our previous average income was. And we are still free to help others with their investments.

"In light of this, I have been running up quite a long distance phone bill and I have found very sympathetic ears. I fact there are a lot of truck drivers who have been on slim rations since Prohibition was ended for the late at night runs that paid so well don't exist. There are also a lot of Teamster leaders who feel a side line of legal and helpful extra income possibilities are very appealing. There are also quite a few friends of those the Feds nailed who think their friends got bum treatment and raps. I expect about a dozen to meet me at Muldoon's Saloon in Grant on Thursday. We can have a few drinks and talk it all over and maybe shoot some pool or play a little poker in the back room. How does this all sound to you?"

Jacob said, "My major concern would be that you and I work hard to avoid doing business with folk that have records of criminal acts or have been in jail. And I've also been thinking that we need to consider legalizing another business and none of the names that are on our Trust have to be used. You see anyone can be an investor. And since those times when we used other names of now deceased men, it might be wise to have a couple new names. But didn't you know a fellow in that foster home named Clarence Abernathy? How about if we used that on any documents relating to new investments?

"And I'm also concerned about Burly. He's been a good help in many ways but he also doesn't understand how close to the edge of the law many politicians and cops and bankers and judges and businessmen come because so much law is screwed up so badly. So I really think it would be best for all three of us if we not take him along. And I already talked to the owner of the Standard Oil station about extra help and he would be glad to give Burly a try and the school also has advertised for a part-time janitor."

Frank referred back to the name change and grinned at his partner as he asked, "How long since you set up our new corporation? And is my thinking like yours regarding naming it Abernathy Associates Incorporated? And I think I know your methods well enough that all our so-called bank loans will be financing it. Also I have a list of names of prospective distributors. And Chief Peter will absolutely not ship any orders without receiving cash for product and shipping so I'm hoping with your phone work we might start out with future cash income almost guaranteed. Now what is your plan for this week?"

Jacob said, "Frank, oops, I mean Clarence, Tuesday I am sending Burly to receive all ten sources of our startup funds. This is not suspicious since he is listed as our Security agent. Look at this map, I've arranged his route to take him farther and farther away from home and ending up in Central City which is about a three hour drive from here. I booked a room for him at the Centralia Hotel and his supper is paid for as well as breakfast in the morning. Of course all his auto expenses are arranged for and he should have a surplus of about $50.00 which is what I told him should tide him over until we send for him to join us or he gets other employment. Then on Wednesday afternoon I'll be going over to Beauford to change our funds into Bearer Bonds requiring either my signature or your new one Clarence which you ought to practice writing. There's one other matter. What about your family?"

"No problem. Gloria and the brats think we'll be going back to Omaha and we'll be getting in touch in a few weeks. But I really like your idea of Atlanta better. And did you get me plenty of film and flashbulbs?"

"Yep. And I still have to get all the mail that's piling up in our postal boxes. I'll see to it Granny receives it after we leave Friday morning. And there's a small shipment of Tonic due to arrive at the station this afternoon which includes a couple cartons each of the three potencies. You'll be able to give samples to our prospective new agents. But I also set it up so that the biggest order with about thirty cartons will arrive at South Fork at about one in the morning on Thursday. Our good friend is more than willing to loan me his Buick so I can run various errands including getting you to your pow-wow. And I am sure there will be no problem getting a ride home for your final night with your family. Then Burly will take our Buick to the station, load all the cartons in it and spend the rest of the night at the South Fork Inn. And again have a surplus after all meals and such are paid. And it will be no problem for you and me to leave by mid-morning."

Both men were thoughtful and silent for a few moments, mulling over the various segments of the week. The family head said, "I feel a bit bad about Granny's health. She's been lookin' poorly and I almost hope our leaving on such short notice isn't too big a strain on her. She's always been kind and fair to us and Gloria and the brats haven't really been any trouble. It's sad that bad things often happen to good people. Oh well, life is full of rocky roads."

Jacob replied, "Hey buddy, you know I don't like to criticize you or tell you what you can do or not do. But we both know you're a lousy gambler and I'm gonna suggest you carry a very small amount of surplus cash. Some of the guests are real sharks when it comes to gambling. And also that you go very easy on the booze and Tonic. We really don't want any scuffles or fights in the tavern that might attract the local gendarmes. And Friday morning we want to empty our deposit boxes. And Mr. Abernathy, it would really be wise as soon as possible to get rid of all those pictures of those under-age females you like so well. It also would be a good idea to get rid of some of those other certificates and documents you like to keep."

Many people were noticing Granny's lessening vitality. She tried to bluster and say how good she felt but she was fooling no one but herself. Wednesday afternoon Gloria and the Doctor confronted her and the man of medicine ordered her to spend a few days in the hospital in which rest and peace and quiet were mandatory. And then she was confined to an oxygen tent with the promise that she could return home in a few days

CHAPTER FOUR

Frank arrived home a little after eight. Gloria met him at the door and touched her forefinger to her mouth and whispered that Maggie was already soundly asleep and Mark had been laying on the couch in the unlighted living room and was already dozing off. Their radio was a floor model and was next to the arm rest of the sofa and playing quietly. The children were both in their bed clothes but the lad had fallen asleep listening to pleasant music. Both of the children's beds were in the same room but he liked it if he was allowed to doze off as the music played.

The woman signaled to her husband to come into the kitchen and then quietly shut the door and spoke very softly, but first she hugged him and held him tightly and they kissed each other. She noticed on his breath the strong odor of whisky and her nose crinkled at the very pronounced smell of stogies. She made no mention of these matters and hurried into a quick mention of their afternoon and evening.

"Honey, I got special permission to take Mark and Maggie to the hospital for a short visit with Granny. We walked there and back and ate supper at about six thirty. The kids were really tuckered out and I made them take a wee bit of your regular tonic after supper so it would be nice and quiet when you got home. I know some of your business meetings can really take a lot out of you. I made meat loaf and I'd be glad to make you a sandwich. And I also baked a coffeecake and a nice batch of cinnamon rolls for you to take with you in the morning."

He spoke quietly back to her. His speech was somewhat slurred. "I had plenty to eat. Muldoon's sets out a good spread. Not hungry for food now. But you know we're heading out to Omaha tomorrow and your pastries would be fine in the morning and to take along in the car."

She asked, "Would you like a cup of coffee?"

"Nope, I want us to be ready for bed." He sat down and cursed his shoelaces and she quickly knelt to undo them and put the shoes away in his closet and his sweaty socks in the hamper. Then he shakily stood and she removed his suit coat and dress tie and hung them on a hanger and then undid his vest and shirt and likewise hung them up. He then ordered her to don her silk night gown. "I want to brush your hair, darling. As quick as you can, sit here by your dressing table."

He asked if her flimsy sleeveless gown was warm enough and she assured him that after her baking the apartment was cozy and once they were under their bedding it would be fine. After she sat on her bench and took out her brush and combs, he stood behind her and gently rubbed her upper arms with his palms and then kissed each of her shoulders. After all he was her husband but she would not ever want anyone else to see her so inadequately clothed.

As Frank gently brushed her hair and stroked her soft tresses he began to whisper to her about the time when he and Jacob would be away. "It's going to take longer than usual because we've been checking into the possibility of buying a home of our own with room for our office and for conferences. And Jacob and I are both sure that Council Bluff, Iowa would be better than Omaha. They're across the Nebraska River from each other but only short drives to any shopping centers with places like Sears or Penny's."

Gloria swiveled around on her bench and almost crushed the man. "You mean we could have a house of our own?"

"Absolutely! But it might take a few months to get everything settled. Jacob and I have seen two big houses which used to offer room and board. They're both two story with an attic and there are bathrooms up and down and I believe both of them have seven bedrooms and both have screened in porches and shade trees. Let me think. There are schools with playgrounds within a few blocks of both houses. And both homes are in churchy neighborhoods which have nicknames of being in the Bible belt. And don't let me forget that both homes have garages and I know your delight, my Dear, of flower gardens. One more thing, the back yards are both fenced in in case the new owner might happen to like the idea of having a dog. Might there be any in my family who might like to have a puppy?"

And Gloria was speechless and jumped up and clung to her man. He embraced her and whispered, "Not a word about this to anyone. We're in the planning stage. And it might require us moving to some other town which could better cause my whole family to be together. But once everything is settled, we can send all the details to you and arrange for a moving van. Hang on with sealed lips. And tell no one. And I need you to do a few things for me before I leave."

"How can I help?"

"I want to start an album of our family pictures like Granny and the O'Connors have. I already have pictures of Burly and Jacob and some of the people we've helped but when I go away I feel lost without your image and the kids to look at. You know I've been using that great newspaper camera and got sharp shots of some of our projects. And I have plenty of film and flashbulbs. So if you would quietly go behind Maggie's crib and lean over the railing and touch her face gently and kiss her forehead, I can get your profile and her little angel face. Then you could go into the living room and softly sit with an arm touching Mark's shoulder and kiss his cheek and again I'll have good shots of your faces and the flashbulbs won't need any room lights on."

Gloria never in public wore garments which like her gown showed more than her throat if she bent forward. Her generation believed in modesty. The exception to this and not usually spoken about in those days between married women were the private moments of married couples. And in the purposely dimmed light she was too naïve to know he was leering at her.

He said, "After we made our vows, we never had a proper honeymoon. It's been awful the way demands of business kept us apart so much. We were entitled to a proper Honeymoon."

"But you've always took good care of us. And after the Justice said we were married you took me in that fancy restaurant and I remember my chicken dinner and mashed taters and corn and biscuits and you let me drink real coffee with cream and sugar and they didn't have regular wedding cake but you had them bring us angel food cake with strawberries and whipped cream. That was the most elegant meal I can remember. I didn't even know then what a honeymoon was but I was never happier in my whole life because you told me you loved me and I knew I'd always love you. And a few days later when you had to go away for several weeks I tried to smile until after you left and I think I cried for more than I ever had in my life."

"Gloria, I guess I've always been too stupid to make it a habit to tell you after we got married that I've always thought you're the prettiest woman I ever knew. I hate to be gone because I'd rather be near you all the time. And I could kick myself over all the times business blocked good honeymoon time. And since I knew tonight would be our last private and intimate time, I bought you a gift that brides are glad to use on a honeymoon. Have you ever seen a negligee such as Frenchmen give their brides? Slip off that silk gown in our bedroom and pose for me and I'll be able to hide pictures away after they're developed and they'll be a private treasure for my eyes only."

Gloria hoped to be less confused but after opening the fancy-wrapped package had even greater consternation. She wondered if the man who had ordered her to do that which was entirely against her character was an evil twin impostor of her husband sent by the devil. She had not removed her gown but had with an angry gesture flung the gift at the man's feet as she opened the bedroom door. The camera flashed just as she came through the doorway.

She spoke softly and just wanted to know how the man she loved could expect her to be so immodest. He snarled at her and replied, "Have you forgotten that I'm the master here and you swore to obey me? Your preacher even instructs all married women to obey their husbands. I am in control here. You will do as I say and I will have some very interesting photos to remind me of you. The founders of this nation were right in keeping control in the hands of the men. Women are next to nothing. Women are here to serve the needs and wants of men and make sure men have all the pleasure they want. Do you understand?"

She answered, "I love you and I do everything I can to make you happy. But Jesus is my Master and I will never do anything that he says is evil."

The man grabbed her hair with his left hand and slapped her across the face with his right palm as he yelled, "Shut your mouth. I'm the only master you've got. You do exactly what I say or I'll see to it you really suffer all of the consequences."

In words of defiance she would later recount as having been her first denial of what he uttered she said, "I don't care what you do to me. I'll always try to put Jesus first."

This infuriated him and he stamped on her left foot and reached for her gown intending to rip it off her so as not to impede his photo session. But her outcry over her hurt foot drove out a cry of pain and before anything else happened the outburst awakened Maggie who began to wail, "Mommy, I'm scared. Mommy! Help me."

In the neighboring O'Connor apartment Dharma was having tea with Mandy Cleveland, the Librarian whose husband worked with records in the city hall. The Cleveland's apartment was the next one down the hall. Bill Cleveland often had to do extra record work whenever one of the city's councils met. And at those times Dharma had happy conversation when Clancy also had things to attend to at the station after his supper. Maureen was soundly asleep and the soon-to-be retired Mandy loved to brag up her grandchildren. Dharma in return loved to tell about happy times in her apartment with Gloria's kids when the Millers happened to go away for a while. But there were a few friends from the station who liked to play Pinochle and it is true that the three kids often got noisy and supposedly broke their card concentration. Both mothers had keys to the other's apartments so either could baby sit and look after the giggly trio as it became necessary.

Dharma was certain the never before noise level in the Miller apartment was a sure indicator of either deliberately caused pain or an accident and she pointed at their phone and its list of urgent numbers and ordered immediate calls to the Police station followed by a call to Dr. Ron Williams upstairs they had just heard going up to bring Nurse Ruth Hillman with him. As she said this she popped the spare key ring off its hook and rushed to swing open Gloria's door.

She entered just as Frank was lowering Maggie's bed rail to easily grab the wee one and flip off her blanket and turned the now weeping child face down as he unbuckled his heavy belt and pulled it free to use as a whip to teach the child to be quiet. But the mother had pulled herself upright and charged into the bedroom to grab his left wrist and yank the belt away as she screamed at him, "No, Frank, no. I'll die before I let you hurt my innocent baby."

The man was totally beyond any rational self-control. "That can be arranged you filthy slut," and twisted her around and shoved her violently through the door. She tripped on a low toy box of Mark's and the raging man stamped on her ankle twisting it to the side. And then he crouched over in back of her and encircled her throat from behind fully ready to squeeze the breath out of her.

But Mark had just been jolted out of his sleep and flew off the sofa and yanked Burly's brass-knobbed walking stick from the hat and coat rack with its place to park canes or umbrellas. As loud as Mark could he screamed that he wouldn't let anyone hurt his sister and charged up behind the maniacal man and swung the brass head of the cane as fiercely as he could aiming to hit the back of the man's head. However his child strength was totally inadequate and the brass end bounced off the right shoulder.

The so-called master of the house was by then pretty numbed by booze and suspicious tonic and he spun around, snatched the cane, broke it over his leg, picked up Mark and threw him at the wall behind the sofa. The child flew against the wall but his hands and arms cushioned the jolt and he fell onto the cushions.

This was the very instant Dharma came charging into the room clicking the switch of the ceiling light. In an instant the tall athletically capable red head saw Maggie cowering, heard Mark moaning, and saw Gloria was crouching with her back to Frank as she tried to get up enough to crawl to her brother. The man was moving his hands toward the young woman's throat and mumbling about finishing the work he started.

Dharma uttered an old Celtic curse she had heard as a child and which had never been explained to her by adults. She concluded by saying shrilly, "Frank, if you so much as touch any of them, I'll break your neck." The man had an instant shiver of fear go through him and he stopped moving and backed away from Gloria to stumble toward the other.

She was almost his height and weight. She wore Levis, a red flannel shirt, and her old comfy riding boots. She roared at the drunk to back off before he got seriously hurt. He hesitated for his blurred vision of her flaming hair and shirt along with her ferocious sound momentarily made him imagine he was confronted by a tigress which any knowledgeable African hunter would warn others to stay as clear as possible of such a deadly killing machine defending its baby. He paused but an instant and then stumbled toward her with his hands outstretched to grab her neck.

The mother slightly crouched and shifted her right foot a bit to the back and also made tight fists of both hands such that her knuckles turned white. Both her arms were slightly bent with fists near her hips. Once the man came almost close enough to reach for Dharma's throat he entered the pain zone. Her right knee came up with shocking speed between his legs doubling him over so that he had no choice but to scream out and try to cup his groin.

Even as his hands were reaching down, the woman's awful right fist came up in a round house blow to the left side of his face that snapped his chin around and bloodied the inside of his cheek as his teeth and flesh collided. He tried to back away and cursed both women calling them both prostitutes at the least and used the worst of gutter language. This was the next to last of the crazed man's mistakes that evening.

Dharma said quite distinctly, "No has ever spoken to me like that without deeply regretting it. And how dare you even think such thoughts about my sweet innocent neighbor?" Then her left fist came around in a blurring arc and smashed into the man's nose breaking it. She was well aware that it was often possible to drive the heel of one's palm against the bottom of the nose so that bone would be driven upward and might pierce the brain possibly causing death.

The man had never before hurt all over so much. But something about his stupid pride and insane rage made him try to grab the woman in a bear hug which had often given him an advantage in beer brawls. She paused until the exactly correct second and her awful right fist drove itself deeply into his abdomen just below his rib cage. He couldn't even begin to get breath and fell down vomiting and gasping as he passed out.

Two police sirens had been heard even as the Tigress had attacked. Garth had gone to the station with Clancy to complete some paperwork and had been roused by the call from Mrs. Cleveland. A second patrol car had been dispatched immediately afterwards. The Marshal and officer came rushing into the Miller apartment less than a minute after Frank went down and out.

Dharma gave her man a perfunctory hug and quick kiss and remarked, "Glory be, isn't it amazing how men never get there until the woman cleans up the mess?"

Garth and Clancy pulled the barely conscious man to his knees, cuffed his hands in back and sat him down on a chair to put a shackle on his ankles. The battered bully regained enough alertness to try to rise out of the chair but the officer with a seemingly nonchalant swing of his night stick connected at the juncture of the man's neck and shoulder and any vestige of awareness was gone.

Dharma quickly snatched a cover off the couple's bed to wrap up the dazed mother and then literally picked her up and set her on the couch propping up her bruised leg on a foot stool. Gloria pulled her brother close to herself and began crooning soft tunes to soothe him. He couldn't suppress all his whimpers but Dharma told him she had never seen a braver lad. Why even in King Arthur's days there couldn't have been braver knights.

Then Dr. Williams arrived with Nurse Hillman. A quick temporary nose job was done to be completed later. The Dr. was concerned that the felon perhaps had internal injuries which should also have attention. He insisted on lab analyses on the tonics. He also ordered that the battered man be taken to the emergency room at the hospital with adequate police attention so that a complete physical would be given him before interment.

But his major attention was for Gloria and the ambulance siren was already heard. The lad and his sister were very lovingly brought to the hospital for necessary remedies and also X-rays. Gloria had been given quick pain relief and was getting very fuzzy before being loaded into the ambulance with Mark. But she rallied just long enough to get Garth's attention.

"Promise me you won't let any of the men hurt Frank. Tell him I really love him. And be sure to tell him I forgive him."

In those last few minutes Dharma had been quickly gathering up some personal items as well as necessary clothing for when Gloria would come home. She also stopped Garth before he headed back to the station and gave him a very gentle hug and a light kiss on the cheek to say thank you on behalf of Gloria.

Granny was not told of the traumatic evenings events and was later told that her granddaughter had tripped over Mark's toy box. She made a mental note to remind both the boy and his sister to be more careful about leaving things out where people could trip over them and perhaps have an accident.   Maggie had no clear memories except she was sure she had been having a very bad dream. Uncle Clancy had very lovingly picked her up and had said, "My little princess, did you have a bad dream? Would you mind spending the rest of the night in Maureen's bed? You can both sleep close to each other and hug your baby dolls so they don't have any bad dreams."

Both Gloria and Frank were unconscious when brought to the hospital. She was carefully checked and her damaged ankle X-rayed. The man was cleaned up and his nose attended to. Hours later the woman roused and was aware of a temporary cast on her ankle. Dr. Williams explained that full recovery could take several weeks and for the first week or so it was mandatory that her mobility would require use of a wheel-chair, but other than that she was in fine condition.

Dr. Williams and a colleague, Dr. Gilbert, conferred with the quite battered man (under police guard) and had bad news for him. His blood pressure was dangerously high as was his rate of pulse and it was certain he had extreme hardening of the arteries. There was also a possibility of liver damage and perhaps worst of all a strong possibility of a brain tumor which was surely responsible for his migraine-related headaches. They learned of the various drugs involved in his "tonic" and that he had been using continually increasing amounts as time went by. All the supposed good that seemed to aid his afflictions had actually been making worse his physical condition and even his tremors.

But the biggest surprise to the physicians was when he candidly admitted that he had maintained his dark brown hair color to the now revealed grayness with dyes. And he also told them that his actual age would become 70 the following February and his real name among about 65 aliases was Harry Hillman. It was also learned that he was sterile and Gloria's pregnancy was most likely the very latest any female could have been impregnated. He told them he was much like the criminal nick-named Baby-face. He had always appeared to be twenty to thirty years younger than his actual age. His speech and dazed answers to many of their questions indicated to the physicians that he was not functioning normally.

There were frequent complaints from others in adjoining cells about the man's often loud mutterings and one insisted he sometimes jabbered in the same way some of the radical "holy rollers" did when supposedly speaking in tongues. But in the morning he seemed completely rational as he insisted he be allowed a private conversation with an attorney. After reading the notes taken by officers of the two women on the scene and the lad's recorded remarks, Frank insisted that all charges against him were absolutely correct and he wished to make a plea of guilty and save the cost of an unnecessary jury trial.

His court-appointed lawyer, James Stillwell, wanted to know what had brought about such a departure from normal procedure. Frank said, "The nearest thing I can explain is that Love broke my heart and turned me around 180 degrees."

The lawyer asked, "Could you please explain this to me?"

"Well, when I got here after the Doctors released me, Marshal Stone told me Gloria insisted he tell me that she loved me. And not only that, but any wrongs I had done to her she forgave. She even insisted that he be sure no one here hurt me. And she knew that the men of this town are ready to do bodily harm to any man who hurts a woman or children. You don't have lynch law here now but it hasn't been so many years since you did."

Attorney Stillwell said, "Could you give me further explanation? There are many felons whose wives declare love but that doesn't explain a radical change of heart."

"You're right. But God and I had a private conversation and He did most of the talking and I did most of the listening."

The counselor requested a summary of his private talk with God in order that a better understanding of his mental state could be had. He was beginning to think there might be a need for a temporary insanity plea which could void the man's assertion of guilt. But Frank was absolutely calm and rational in his words and demeanor.

"God said to me a whole bunch of statements I have heard from various preachers who used Bible phrases. He told me He loved every person in the world and gave His only Son who was sinless to die for them. He mentioned how that even as Jesus was dying he prayed for God's forgiveness for sinners. He mentioned how that he even promised a thief who deserved to die that they would both be together in

Heaven. He told me how His only Son died for the sins of the world and also rose again and promised he was coming back. And He let me know for sure that He had been forever sending His love to me through His people such as Gloria who was full of forgiveness and always tried to do good for me and even wanted to be sure the other prisoners didn't hurt me."

At this point the old man's hands began to shake and he started to moan about head pain and soon pitched forward holding his head and slumped onto the interrogation table. Dr. Williams had stopped in the station to give a written report to the Sheriff and was immediately called by the lawyer. Medicine was quickly administered to prevent a seizure and ease the pain. Within about fifteen minutes the man straightened up and resumed his conversation with the attorney as if there had been no interruption.

"And I knew somehow that Jesus would accept me like he did that felon on the cross if I believed He was God's only son and I would really be sorry for all my lifetime of sins and really wanted to be different than I was all my life. I begged him to accept me and I told Him I didn't want to be like that anymore. And all at once I had peace like I never knew there could be and I felt clean inside for the first time in my life. And Mr. Stilwell, will Jesus do this for anyone who comes to him? Do you understand all I've said? Have you ever asked him to do the same for you about receiving you and forgiving you?"

The lawyer was not a very vocal person about religious matters but admitted that as a Baptist who accepted the Bible as God's truth he would never deny the reality of God's work in lives. Yet he had also heard people headed for trial who pushed religion as an argument for leniency. However Frank's words carried the ring of reality and would have to be carefully evaluated.

The man had only accepted strong coffee and orange juice for breakfast after being given a strong dose of painkiller to keep the worst edge off his ominous headache. "I know there is no way I can ever pay my debt to society or give even a slightly fair payback to the dozens Jacob and I cheated. But I am hoping Marshal Stone might be able to put me in close touch with one of Mr. Hoover's agents to at least catch my partner in crime and prevent any more evilness."

The arrested felon asked for a chance to lay down to give medication time to ease the head pain and tremors before the Marshal came back from the courthouse office of Federal Agent Norris Smith who brought along a stenographer to record all conversations. The first thing the Agent did was to show record of several names of possessors of the fingerprints the Sheriff's staff had sent in the previous evening. Since the turn of the century use of prints by law enforcement agencies such as Scotland Yard, there had never been any such duplication and it was believed that it was impossible.

Frank explained that he had been printed several times but in each case he had been using an alias except the previous night when his current name was involved. "I got taken in for being drunk and disorderly about ten years ago in Milwaukee. It turned out that several witnesses in the tavern said that I was fighting in self-defense and the fellow who started it was an officer out of uniform who had a reputation for starting brawls. His Captain had him locked up and all I had to do was to sleep it off and there was no fine. My alias was Robert Stein."

Frank soon begged that he be allowed to have a cot brought into the interrogation room with extra pillows to prop his head up which did much to somewhat alleviate his pain and tremors. And he repeatedly would have short periods when he dozed off briefly and when alert had frequent blanks in his memory and considerable repetition. But the main theme of all his testimony had to do with Agent Smith and police investigation to prove his criminal behavior and duplicity with Jacob Ebner as they had schemed over and over as con men to greatly reduce the financial assets of their victims.

He insisted that the Sheriff and Mayor exercise their responsibilities as Trustees of the joint trust regarding thorough inspection of safe deposits. And he also said they ought to immediately also check all deposits and checking accounts that Jacob controlled and which he had promised were going to be put into higher interest-paying accounts. It was quickly discovered that all accounts of Granny, Gloria, Burly, and the two scoundrels had been closed and all the amounts put into bearer bonds cashable only by Jacob who was now gone from town.

The safe deposit boxes showed nothing incriminating regarding Burly Dodge whom Frank insisted had never been involved in anything even slightly unlawful. His box contained inexpensive small souvenirs and post cards from various places to which he had taken the guilty duo.

Frank's box had albums of innocent pictures of women he and Jacob had beguiled and swindled. But other albums had pictures of all the girls he had seduced and apparently he drugged or intoxicated them and then took shameful photos of them when they were unconscious. Almost without exception every female had been offered matrimony but the few that agreed had been tricked by false documents and presumably had wedding vows under the auspices of fake justices-of-the peace. The man had never been married and only twice had there been pregnancies. And as the time of interrogation continued the man seemed to be having more and more lapses of memory until there was only a small number of his photographs which he recognized although each photo had the name and home town listed.

Jacob's box was claimed by the Mayor and Sheriff ahead of the fleeing thief and the ledger clearly showed the extent of the loss of money of almost everyone who ever had done business with the two con artists. There would be sad news for all the trustees of the newly constituted combined trust for there was not one penny in any of their accounts. Then additional examination of Jacob's box revealed the names of all the banks from which so-called construction loans had been paid in which Granny (Hester Sue Brown) had apparently been the applicant using her property as security. She had been duped into signing a multitude of loan applications with a combined total of almost four times her property's appraised value. Burly had been the approved messenger who had received bearer bonds which he had delivered to Jacob.

Intermixed in Frank's delivery of information to Agent Smith were snippets which showed their modus operandi with those whom they bilked. First there came a review of recent prominent area newspapers as to obituaries. Also a check of county records as to wedding dates, birthdates of children, and dates of deaths. Next came condolence visits and sometimes cemetery visits with a floral gift. Attendance at the church of the bereaved was almost mandatory. A gradual buildup of social connections such as lunch or visits to places the bereaved liked to visit were greatly promoted. And during the continued contacts there came many repairs in which Burly took care of necessary maintenance. But all the types of contacts with the widows who were never in bad financial shape came with little suggestions as to how it would be possible to increase income by judicial small investments. The duo never promoted risky outlays of resources and made sure the returns were always at higher percentages than other bank or commercial institutions. Then when they finally left, they made sure the widows would not be in desperate straits and thus would be expecting additional returns which never came.

The saddest part of all the chicanery was not found out until after Frank's arrest and Jacob's disappearance a few hours later for mail sent to the large Miller post office box was delivered on Monday. Channeled through the so-called Treasurer arrived eviction notices to all the renters and tenants from the banks which jointly were owed four times the market value of Granny's estate. Checks which had been sent out late including those to the Phone Company, Gas Company, Coal Company, water works, and Electric Company had all bounced. But most of the inhabitants were paid up through the end of the year according to their own receipts and also according to a little notebook of Granny.

One of Frank's biggest concerns was how his deserted former partner had planned to bilk Mrs. Pulaski regarding the sale of her Buick. It was to have been the getaway machine and loaded with thousands of dollars of tonic. With all the papers the widow had signed it would have been no trouble to sell the auto or even trade it for a less conspicuous vehicle such as a truck with a covered box or perhaps a delivery van. Once out of state, it would be hard to quickly trace what had really happened. But Frank was actually totally in the dark as to where Jacob was headed. The last area his foggy memory held was Omaha but he asserted that it was much more likely the escape route would be southward.

About a week later it was learned for sure that the swampy end of Georgia was the fatal destination. Apparently the too-wise swindler planned to change his payoff amount from relatives of Prohibition crime bosses and was actually pursued by their associates and finally caught in the Okeefenokee Swamp near the Suwannee River. The rear end of the car was riddled with bullet holes and both tires shredded. One of the 38 revolvers was still in the car, all shots having been fired. The front end of the car was caved in against a tree. A fire had started as bottles of the alcohol-enriched tonic had shattered and ignited. There had been no salvageable tonic and all luggage was scorched. The fleeing man had left behind bloodstains which led into the swamp but no trace of him or any contents of his cash box was ever found. Had he survived any bullet wounds it seemed totally unlikely he had lasted very long.

Gloria and Mark were brought home Friday morning while Frank was conferring with Hoover's agent. The woman had been strictly ordered to be using a wheelchair for a week or so. Burly and Garth carried her in her chair up to her apartment and there was a joyful reunion with Maggie and the O'Connors. Granny was brought home on Saturday afternoon, October 8th. By then the mail sack had been delivered and the retired couple, Fred and Sandy Epps, volunteered to sort it out for the proper recipients.

There was quite an uproar and complaint to Mayor Bernard Stillwell over the threatened evictions which supposedly were due by Monday November 1st. All of the renters had valid receipts up to the end of the year verified by entries found in Granny's personal ledger. However Gloria had no receipts since the rent for her apartment and the double room of Burly and Jacob were presumably covered by janitorial work by Burly. Marshal Stone's rent was paid through the end of October.

But a worse shocker to Gloria was that long overdue payments on much of the furniture in her apartment made them all due for repossession on Friday, October fifteenth. The carpet, sofa, end table, radio, easy chair and ottoman, lamps, dining room table and chairs, and the brass bed and crib were due to be removed. Mark's bed was a fold-up rollaway which had been a gift from Granny which would stay as well as Gloria's dressing table and stool. And of course all bedding and clothing and personal items would stay. Frank's possessions had yet to be ruled on.

Since there had been a plea of guilty on all counts a hearing before Judge Nehemiah Stillwell was scheduled for Friday afternoon at four. He would then determine the sentence which was vastly expanded due to the attempted murder of the woman who had been supposed to be his wife. It was expected to be a prison term of at least twenty years. And considering that the physicians were doubtful that the man could survive only as much as a couple of years, arrangements were already being made to incarcerate the man at the Illinois Joliet penitentiary at which he could receive hospital care.

Clancy told her about the man's claim to now be a person who wished to please Jesus and really was sincerely repentant even though there was very little he could do beyond sharing everything he could with Hoover's agents to help prevent other such things from happening.

And Gloria was now in the throes of anxiety and began to wonder if all the grief and uncertainty of what her future seemed to hold could be real. Was she in a nightmare that couldn't possibly be reality? Where was God now? What had she done wrong to invite overwhelming trouble? She tried to pray and Jesus' words came to her that she should fear not for he was with her and would never forsake her. And there was a spark of hope that her Shepherd who never failed had plans for her and the children that right then she couldn't even imagine and that all would come together for their greater good. And she then prayed that Frank had really come to know the Lord. She also knew she had to visit him and say farewell but she would never give him a parting kiss.

After lunch Burly recruited Garth to assist in bringing the woman to the jail with her wheelchair for a visit with the prisoner. She hardly recognized him for the cleansing at the hospital had removed his hair color and the jail clothes were completely different from his customary dapper clothes. The bandage on his nose also made him difficult to recognize. He was held to the prisoner's chair by handcuffs to the arm rests. Both table and chair were bolted to the floor.

Garth wheeled her up to the table and with just a nod to the felon left closing the door. The room had windows on two sides allowing observation of the visitor and prisoner but quiet conversations could not be heard by observers. The man nodded to the woman and quietly said, "Thank you so much for coming to see me, Sweetheart."

The slight smile which had been on her face hardened almost to a frown and she held up her right hand with forefinger pointed toward the ceiling much as a teacher would with an unruly student and waved it slightly from side to side in a forbidding move. "I am not your sweetheart nor will I stay to talk to you should you use any other such expressions. I know now I am not nor have I ever been your wife since you tricked me. I am Miss Gloria Brown and our daughter is Miss Margaret Brown and my brother is Master Mark Brown. Miss Brown is an acceptable way to address me. But I did hear something good about you that I hope is true. I have hoped for years that you might somehow come to trust Jesus as your Lord and Savior because too many things didn't add up right."

The woman listened intently as he repeated what he had told his attorney. He said, "I still feel bad about all the grief I've caused others and especially you. But after all these years I have a clear conscience. But I really want to assure you of how sorry I am for anything I've done that hurt you. And the fact that you still had love for me in spite of everything and made it clear you forgave me were the sharpest instruments God used to illustrate to me that it was all just like his Son."

The woman felt as if she was in the presence of a new person who was already beginning to cling to the One who made new creations out of old sinners. And she told him she had brought to the jail his reading glasses and a copy of the Bible. In return he told her that aside from film taken from his camera all the other film and flashbulbs and carrying case were hers as was his entire wardrobe which he was sure he'd never need again. He begged her to give his deepest apologies to Mark and she replied that the lad had already expressed an attitude of forgiveness.

The man ended the time allotted for their visit by saying, "Miss Gloria Brown, please pray for me and as I learn to pray I'll be praying for you and the children and as my memory permits for all those who have been so kind. And I want you to know that I already believe that God is beginning to prepare to smooth out the bumpy roads that face you. I am sure people will come your way that will help you in any hours of need. And I won't be surprised if in the years to come some decent man may meet you who will consider you to be and have all the things I was too blind to see. You deserve better than I could ever have done for you."

It has been often said that free speech and freedom of the press were two of the bulwarks along with freedom of religion of fundamental American freedom. But there have always been those that abused these basic rights to attain their own agendas. And among the worst were newspapers that constantly sought out the dirt and downgraded good people and organizations. Such sensationalist "rags" love to use expressions such as "it is alleged," or "a reliable witness who must remain anonymous," or "how come this has been covered up?" One of these publications was the Crawford Sentinel which always claimed to give the whole truth, but usually loved to tell that which was scandalous, suspicious, and seldom had much good to say about public figures or well-liked citizens.

The Sentinel was a weekly sheet which usually came out early on Saturdays. The caption on the lead article was "What Popular Waitress Has Been Living In Sin?" There was then without any identification talk about an illegitimate baby and failure of any law enforcement to enforce the law. There was even mention of the action by government employees to overlook taking action to straighten out crooked politics in what used to be a law-abiding town.

CHAPTER FIVE

Granny's actual birth date had never been recorded in Stillwell County records for her birth preceded the keeping of such records. The date had been entered into the old family Bible but a leaky roof in the cabin had allowed rain to soak the Bible and had washed away the old ink. But it was quite correct as to the day and month, not the year. She was sure she was well into her eighties and she was becoming more and more aware of her failing strength and health which had been the reasons for her short hospital stay and use of the oxygen tent.

Those who had known her for many years held in their minds that she was one of the last remaining Pioneer Women. To them she was the embodiment of the traits which were most closely related to such ladies. First and foremost was her staunch faith in God and her desire to always stay as close to Jesus' leading as she possibly could. Secondly was how her daily dealings with those around her, be they good or bad people, exhibited a gentleness and kindness like her Savior. Next were her work ethic and her stick-to-it-iveness to get things done.

The old lady had been completely checked as to blood pressure, pulse, fever, respiration and other related matters soon after entry into the hospital. Necessary medications to bring all these to safe levels had been administered and with them a regimen of sedatives to keep her calm and restful as well and also to keep her drowsy and to encourage more sleep than was usual.

Thus when the chirp of an ambulance's siren came in the later evening on Thursday, it caused Hester Sue to become alert and she had to know what was going on. As quickly as nurses had been able to prepare the then unconscious Gloria for an ankle X-Ray prior to having her leg brought into proper position for a short term temporary cast, Dr. Williams popped in to see Granny.

He tersely reassured her that the children were both safe and that in Maggie's darkened room her granddaughter had tripped over Mark's toy box and had a bad sprain which would require the use of a wheel chair for a few days but there was no permanent damage. He had concluded with a slight scolding for the old lady for she had not yet taken her sleeping pills for the night. She in exchange took the pills and then softly chided the medicine man about how come they always wanted to wake people up to take pills to sleep.

He had concluded, "You'll have to take that up with the management but I gotta go now. Tomorrow afternoon you'll learn all the details. But for now it's sleepy time."

She was roused for breakfast Friday morning and after the dishes were cleared away she insisted the tray be left so she could rest her big Bible on it and her bed be left tilted up so she could read. As had been her normal wakeup ritual she had whispered, "Good morning, Father. Thank you for the rest you gave me and the food they're bringing. Bless it and them and me, amen."

She had turned to Psalm one and then to the twenty third. They were both near the top of her list of favorite portions. She had then gone to the account of the Resurrection morning and smiled at how God had used women to bring the good news to the disciples. She had then again begun to feel drowsy and had a nurse remove the tray and her Bible. As she entered again into a time of sleep she had a thought that she would soon be going home.

Late in the afternoon she distantly heard familiar voices and came back to full alertness in time to greet two visitors, Sheriff Caleb Strait and his wife Ellen. She was not particularly surprised for in the back of her mind she had been quite sure that bad news was coming. It had not been a premonition, but there had been a load of niggling suspicions that all had not been well. She told them both that there had been little things which had made her very curious. But she had no fear for her Heavenly Father always had the final say and her Savior always guarded his sheep.

She bade them slide two chairs close to her tented bed and cheerfully greeted them. From her facial expressions any that saw her would have thought that nothing was bothering her but in truth she could not remember ever having felt weaker. Her body was telling her that she was far worse off than she could ever remember.

Before Caleb could begin to relate the events of the recent hours she smiled brightly and said, "All is well with my soul. Nothing you tell me can give me fear or worry. The Apostle Peter's words are perfect for me for with him I can say I have joy unspeakable and full of glory. I have never felt my Lord's presence closer than right now. So whatever you have to tell me will only make me more ready for Him to take me home"

With as few words as possible he recounted the totally unexpected encounter between the man and his supposed wife. He skipped the camera expectations of the man and never spoke of what had later been seen in the degrading albums of young girls. He mentioned the frightening of Maggie and how she had been allowed to consider it a bad dream. He had a hard time controlling his anger over the ankle damage. He praised Mark who had used every bit of his childish strength to protect Gloria his older sister. And then he also told of his astonishment over how Dharma had thrashed the man.

Ellen interjected that if she had been there, she would have joined Dharma's attack even though she had never tried to hurt any man. She added that if a U.S. Marshal could do so for children he ought to pin a medal on the boy. Granny commented on how it was certain that her grandson was much like Handsome Harry his grandfather and very close to the brave character of his father who had given his life attempting to save lives on Lake Michigan.

As Caleb resumed the further events concerning Frank Miller up to his sentencing and the order to send him to the Joliet Prison, Granny stopped the narration upon hearing of the felon's conversion. She said, "I always hoped he did really have faith and I've been praying for him to be genuinely born again since Gloria and him got hitched up. So we gotta praise the Lord it happened before it was too late. But I feel awful that they deceived all of us with a fake wedding certificate."

After the Sheriff told her of the total theft of all assets of the individuals who had previously thought the new Trust would be safe, and then broke the sad news to her that vast loans to ten banks made by them had replaced all ownership in any property, Granny was silent for a couple of minutes and had a quite solemn look on her face. Then suddenly a brilliant smile shed all trace of consternation and she began to chuckle.

She said, "Ellen and Caleb, don't worry about me or feel bad. I didn't bring anything into this world when I came and I sure won't take anything with me when I leave. And I heard a saying that instead of worrying Granny oughtta pray and leave the worrying to God. And I know my Jesus can keep every one of them safe after I'm gone. And the preacher has often told us that as we keep on doin' what the Lord wants us to we're layin' away treasure in Heaven where no thief can touch it. I think it might be soon when I see my Shepherd face to face and I'm gonna be able to kneel before him and lay any treasure at his feet."   The visiting friends were almost ashamed of their own degrees of faith when compared with the unshakable trust and confidence of the ailing matriarch. The Sheriff said a brief prayer for his elderly sister before they left and after Granny's supper she was soon deeply asleep.

Granny after breakfast and final medical procedures was ordered to ride home in an ambulance. It was late Saturday morning when she was finally situated at her the table for tea and some chicken broth which had been readied for her arrival by Sandy Van Epps and Mandy Cleveland. Fred Van Epps and Bill Cleveland had joined forces to sort out the large bag of mail which had been held back by Jacob until he had departed.

The grand dame would not admit to fatigue and aches which were her personal warning flags that she could not expect life to go on very long. But she did admit to the helpful ladies that she considered the Crawford Sentinel which had been dropped off unwanted had far less value than sale-priced toilet paper. She declared that when Jesus returned no lies or other sins would exist.

Although there was no money available to Miss Gloria Brown from any bank accounts she did have a few dollars of grocery money in her purse and both of the children offered her their meager collection of coins from their little treasures. She was deeply touched by their concern that she might need what pittances they had, however she assured them they ought to be saving what they had for Christmas shopping. But she also showed them the money taken from her former husband and turned over to her by his lawyer.

Uncle Burly volunteered a ride to the IGA for Gloria and both children before Granny was brought home. The wheel chair could be folded up and the spacious Buick had plenty of room. At the store Mark and Maggie proudly wheeled her around and Burly pushed the grocery cart and did the reaching for high articles. The young woman had always taken a list with her and never bought treats such as cookies which she or Granny could bake. But she did get one luxury item, a bag of red and white peppermints for little treats.

It was well into the afternoon when the shoppers arrived home and quickly put way their loads. And then after what had seemed like a minor eternity, it was possible to welcome Granny home. The ladies had assisted her to get to the toilet and wash up afterwards for she was quite weak in her legs and also had a degree of dizziness. Then she insisted she just leave on her clothes minus her shoes and wear her quilted bath robe for she could not seem to get warm even under her blankets and lap robe.

The children assisted in putting her lap tray with its short legs on her legs after Gloria put extra pillows behind her back. Then the mother brought in a mug of chamomile tea seasoned with honey and lemon as directed and arranged old photos of early family days on the dresser where light from the lamp on her table made them very easy to see. Next Granny's box of stationery and envelopes and a couple of fountain pens were set on her tray after the tea was gone.

It was very obvious to Gloria that her Granny was close to exhaustion and she ordered Mark to prepare to push her back to their apartment. But from those hidden resources all grandparents seem to somehow have to hug the little ones there came forth surprisingly strong hugs as the children leaned over her bed. And she also had to speak briefly to each of them.

"Maggie, my little angel, never stop being kind and always obey your Mama. And Mark, I am so proud of you. You have the same kind of courage as your Daddy and Grandpa and no soldier could ever have been braver. Finally, Gloria, I'm gonna leave a note for you and I am going to ask Garth to give it to you. And I'm not gonna avoid getting my sleep by making up a list for you. You know how I love lists. And I'll never stop loving any of you. Now scat. I got words to put on paper I gotta get written and then a long night of sound sleep."

Gloria first inquired about an evening meal for Granny since it was time for supper and insisted the tray have the writing encumbrances moved to one side so she could eat some apple sauce and a chicken salad sandwich and another cup of tea which was almost more than she wanted. She again embraced the children and Gloria and dismissed them so she could to do her writing. But first she asked that a notice be left on the lobby chalkboard requesting Marshal Garth see her for a few minutes when he arrived.

The Brown matriarch had just finished her writing when the man politely rapped on her door and responded to her invitation. He moved a chair close to her bed and listened carefully to her quiet words.

"Son, I have a little letter for Gloria I want you to give her after I'm gone and the final prayers are said. Use your best judgment as to the best time. And no objections that I might be down here a long time. Tain't so. I'm ready to go home and my ticker and lungs are just about worn out. And most of my strength is gone but I can still see you and the photos on the dresser. So just listen up. And after I've said my piece you can give me them two pills and a swig of grape juice.

"Temptations will come but Never Give in. And so will hard days when hope seems almost gone but Never Give Up. The Holy Spirit will always see to it God's Word will keep you from givin' in or givin' up. Those words apply to both of you.

"And the Lawyer told me that when the banks foreclose they can only take the building and land but none of the contents. So all personal property is safe and nothing can be taken unless it's fastened like cupboards and light fixtures and plumbing fixtures.

"In my note I told Gloria It's my wish for her to keep my cedar chest which has my wedding gown and veil all kept safe by moth balls and cedar shavings and her mother and me was the only two to use the gown but she can save it for when Maggie gets wed. And there's a big seaman's trunk for when she moves. There's also my bookcase with my photo albums and all my recipe books and filing cards. And she also ought to take my old foot treadle sewing machine and never forget my rocker and quilt or the mantle clock and any pictures hanging on the wall.

"And there are cans and boxes of food and all the tools in the basement and the washin' machine and beds and cloth goods and such in the rooms and all my clothes what'll be left and cook stoves and fridges and all the cookin' stuff and silverware and dishes and none of it is going to the banks. There are loads of needy people who could benefit from everything that'll be left behind what Gloria will want to give away or maybe sell real cheap and you and Burly can help her decide. Will you make me a solemn promise to help my dear girl when the time comes?"

The man rose to his feet and stood at attention and raised his hand as witnesses do in court and he said, "I solemnly promise and may God help me to do my very best." He then gave her the last two pills and a sip of juice and quickly removed her tray and the extra pillows which had propped her up.

She was already sliding into sleep but she had enough breath to whisper, "Granny loves you, Son. Give me a good night kiss." He leaned over her and touched his lips to her cheek but he was certain she had already slipped into a deep slumber. He planned to ask Dr. Williams to check her after she had a few hours to sleep.

Garth got very little restful sleep when he finally quit doing mostly unneeded tasks in his room. He had never met his own grandparents and the old lady and her wise advice that he must never give in and never give up dominated his thoughts and that she had from her first meeting with him had treated him as if he was another part of her family. He had the awful feeling that she would very soon be leaving earth but he knew she was totally ready to enter Heaven. And he felt honored that she had requested a kiss.

The Dr. was just leaving Granny's room as Burly and Garth came downstairs. He signaled them both to remain silent and to bring Gloria over in her wheel chair but to request that she come with them and not just then tell the children that Granny was gone but she had passed without any outward indications of suffering.

Gloria knew immediately that something was seriously wrong as she invited both of the honorary uncles to stick around for a few minutes so she could make up more batter so all could have pancake breakfasts. Burly said, "Sound's great, Honey but it's best if I just stay with the kids and you let Garth wheel you to Granny's room. He can explain."

But no explanation was needed as the young woman saw Dr. Williams standing outside her grandmother's room accompanied by Nurse Ruth Hillman. Both of them had very solemn expressions and the Dr. whispered a couple of things to his nurse who quickly went to the office phone to make a couple of hushed calls.

He then bent down in front of the young mother and gently held both of her hands as he said, "I wish there was an easy way to tell you but there isn't. A few hours ago while she slept peacefully, God called her home. There was no evidence of pain and her face was totally tranquil and there was even a light smile on her face. But I knew and so did she when she came home that her hours were numbered. There was nothing more I could have done and I knew her well enough that I was sure she would have rejected any further treatment.

"Ruth is placing calls to Rev. Michaels who should be here very quickly. And the undertaker Mr. Charles Beakman who owns Beakman Burials won't be long either. It is my understanding that Granny made arrangements with him for this very day after your Grandfather Harry's funeral."

She slid her hands out of the soft touch of the man's fingers and pulled her apron up to wipe her now wet cheeks. She said very softly, "May I please see her for just a minute or two?"

Garth wheeled her in next to the bed. She straightened up as if to move closer and her right ankle in its cast could not support her and she began to fall forward but the strong Marshal quickstepped to her side and caught her right elbow as he also reached around her waist and pulled her close to support her. She forced herself to bend enough to reach the cold cheek for a final kiss and whispered barely audibly, "Good bye, Granny." She then turned away and clung to Garth and wept audibly with her head on his shoulder and tears soaking his shirt next to his neck.

After her tears became moderate she slid back onto the wheel chair and mopped her face with her apron and said

"Thank you, Garth. You were right there when I needed someone strong and kind. And I hope you can forgive me for soaking your shirt. I'll be glad to wash and dry and iron it for you later."

"Don't even let it enter your thoughts. I still have three shirts on hangers in my room. But I will accept your offer of pancakes." And just about then her pastor and his wife came in the back way and met her as Garth wheeled her out. They each knelt at her sides and held her hands and offered up a gentle prayer for her and the children but said very little except short condolences. She thanked them and assured the minister she was planning on normal Sunday school and Church attendance, which Granny would expect of them.

Mr. Beakman, the undertaker drove up in his limo followed by the Beakman Burials hearse. As is typical of most such services, the utmost dignity and polite silence prevailed as the remains of the departed soul's body were transported away. Mr. Beakman told Gloria that her Grandmother had many years earlier completely prepared the order of service and the young lady was also informed that after Granny's husband's funeral the widow set up a joint savings plan payable only after her death to Beakman Burials.

"Miss Brown, Hester Sue deposited small amounts every month since then and after every expense of her funeral is paid, there should be between forty and fifty dollars which is to be used entirely at your discretion. And I would like to advise that the service be held on Wednesday so it can be announced adequately. I'm sure you and your Pastor can work the details out.

"Oh! One more thing to do: if you could make arrangements for her burial clothes to be brought to us this afternoon it would be greatly appreciated. And I want you to know that my wife and I also grieve with you and your family. She was a grand lady, one in a million."

Gloria took a few ragged breaths and again wiped her face with her apron after the undertaker and the Michaels left and then said, "Garth, there's no way I can thank you enough for how you stayed close and moved me around when I felt so alone. I can't express how important your gentleness and kindness are to me. And now would you bring me to tell Dharma and Clancy before we get those pancakes cooking?"

When she told her neighbors about Granny's departure to live in God's land, the strong cop began to sob and bent down to give her a huge shoulder hug and a kiss on the cheek. The dangerous defender of the one who had given birth on the same day and afterwards considered to be her younger sister knelt down to embrace Gloria and whispered that she and her husband and little Maureen loved Granny too but they'd wait until after their breakfast to tell their daughter the happy sad news.

Burly was humming an off-key tune and busy enlarging the bowl of batter under the watchful eyes of the pajama, robe, and slippered ones who were giggling at the twisted faces the man made as he sloppily stirred the concoction he was almost ready to begin frying. The returning pair could easily detect the grief he couldn't hide but had tried to disguise.

Garth shooed him away from the stove and told him to wash his hands before he got sticky batter all over everything. "I've spent years camping with my dad and he taught me everything there is to know about cooking flapjacks. So we ain't gonna let a wheel-chair Mama near the skillet this time."

Mark asked if they could see Granny after they ate and got ready for church. Gloria told the children they couldn't. Then Maggie chimed in, "Is she still sick, Mama?" "Not even a tiny bit, dear." Mark said, "So we kin see her before church?" "No. We can't visit her. She's not here now." Maggie asked, "Well who is she visiting?" The astute lad said, "Sis, she's with the Heavenly Father in his land now and Jesus promised all God's children that he would see to it every one of us would have beautiful homes up there." The little girl's next question was as to whether they couldn't ride the train up there so they could visit Granny.

Burly pulled his chair close to the tall dinner chair and put an arm around his precious sweetheart and very softly explained to her that God would call his children by name when it was time for them to come home to his city and it might be that his angels brought them there but he admitted no one knew for sure just how God did it or when it would be.

Although the pancakes with syrup were every bit as luscious as usual, none of the appetites were even close to normal and the atmosphere at the table was much quieter than was normal with almost no joviality. The men did do the dishes and straightening up in the kitchen and then both hurried to their rooms to put on their customary Sunday worship garments. They all met again in the apartment and dawdled a bit for they were considerably early to leave for Church.

Gloria had been thinking about her friend Heidi and was glad she had a few minutes in the office to call the

Dahlgrens and share Granny's departure with them and also to request help after dinner to prepare burial clothes to bring to the Beakman Burials premises. The young woman tried to fill her head with details which sometimes helped ease the emptiness of her heart. She was also very glad for the presence of Garth and Burly to serve as wheelchair navigators once they got to the back steps of Granny's Lodging or the front steps of the Good Shepherd Lutheran Church.

The church had just begun the habit of preceding the worship service with Sunday school for all ages. The adults who came for the time of Bible teaching met in the sanctuary and children up to senior high school had room for classes in the church basement. When all gathered together for worship (from which preschoolers and those in the lower grades were excused before the sermon for a time of children's church) the only major difference was the inclusion of an extra sheet in the bulletin which told of Granny's demise and the announcement of visitation hours and the time and place of the funeral.

The First Baptist Church which had one of the biggest congregations in Stillwell had the greatest seating capacity and also the largest fellowship hall for weddings, funerals, and such. It also had a huge amount of parking space and was only about a quarter mile from the Lutheran church. Their Pastor, Melvin Bradshaw, was about ten years younger than Rev. Michaels and he and his wife Selma had three pre-school children. In the six years he had been pastoring there had been a steady growth in the congregation and the younger man had also gotten acquainted with most other pastors at monthly prayer gatherings.

Thus it was no surprise that the funeral was set for Wednesday at eleven followed by a luncheon. The Baptist Pastor and many of his flock had been well acquainted with the deceased and friendships abounded between both congregations. Tuesday afternoon and evening and briefly before the funeral on Wednesday were designated as visitation times.

The young Pastor began the service by welcoming all and then led in a brief prayer. He told briefly of an ecumenical conference he and his wife had once attended and mentioned their acquaintance with married Salvation Army officers. "We chanced to dine with them and discussed church matters including funerals. We were told that it was quite common that deaths of believers were spoken of as Promotions to Glory and that even though grief and sorrow were normal; the meetings were considered as celebrations. And today we are celebrating the joyful life of our dear Sister and a number of folks are going to share experiences they have had with her.

"In keeping with her expressed desires, an offering is going to be received after the service for Granny's favorite charity. One of her greatest passions was that children must never be abused or neglected, nor should unfortunate widows or deserted mothers. She has on several occasions mentioned to me the magnificent work being done by Nazarene churches around the country on behalf of orphans and many young mothers. The Nazarene denomination has for decades attempted to do what they could to provide desperately needed help. Their closest facility is in the county south of us where they were able to obtain a school building badly in need of repairs such that a new school was going to be built in a better location. Money poured in from many denominations to help and volunteers have renewed the old decrepit building which does have a gym and a dining hall and adequate sleeping space for those who need them the most. Their motto is that no child or needy mother should be neglected and the name of the facility is The Good Shepherd Shelter. Granny sent them whatever she could and this church and the Lutheran Church as well as many others do what they can. Any thing you can spare including pennies will be blessed of God to support this noble work."

It was never mentioned that the almost fifty dollars surplus of the funeral account would be applied and even Gloria's children added pennies and nickels to make it an exact fifty. The grand total which came in was almost a hundred dollars and not one penny would be wasted by the frugal Nazarenes.

Granny had years before laid out an order of service which no one expected to alter. Her favorite hymns were A Mighty Fortress Is Our God, The Old Rugged Cross, and Amazing Grace. These were interspersed throughout the service to be sung by the mourners and in between them came shared accounts of friends. The Scripture readings were read responsively. Amongst them were the twenty third Psalm and the Beatitudes.

Rev. Michael's sermon title was taken directly from Granny's last note to Gloria which he had shown her pastor. NEVER GIVE IN AND NEVER GIVE UP. He gave a clear gospel presentation stressing that giving in to the Devil would take you to Hell but believing in Jesus' death, burial, and resurrection and then giving in to him meant salvation and forgiveness which the strength given by the Holy Spirit could cause you to never give in to loss of hope. He asked for a time of silent prayer so people could be assured of eternal life.

Garth and Burly carried Gloria in her chair to the fellowship hall in the lower level of the church and she and the children were first to get their lunch. Many from both churches and also friends from several others had brought platters of sandwiches, potato salad, fruit bowls, and dessert items. And almost everyone who stayed for lunch had at least paused to offer condolences and words of encouragement to the bereaved.

But the hardest part of all was the actual graveside conclusion back at the Lutheran church's grave yard behind the church. This part of it all was least attended and to Mark and Margaret it gave the reality of finality. The gentle and kindly pastor's wife took them aside to give them easy to understand words.

"Children, just a few Sundays ago your teachers told you how God made everything. He separated the water and the earth and made all the plants and animals and all the strength He had put in the ground brought life to all the plants and animals. Then He did something very special and from the earth made the body of a man and breathed life into it. And now when He invites people to come live with Him in Heaven, we put their dead bodies back in the ground until Jesus comes again and He makes them rise again so they will have perfect bodies living forever in their forgiven souls."

The very simple lesson was quite understandable to Mark but Maggie for many days had questions which needed repeat explanation. And Gloria did not wish to be alone and stayed close to Garth and Burly and also tried to think through the disposal of all the things which would not be left behind when the days of eviction came. She craved closeness particularly of good adult friends, such as the O'Connors and the Dahlgrens.

And after receiving the several weeks old announcement from the furniture company that they could no longer put off their recovery of things purchased by a large loan with continually delinquent payments, it was realized that Thursday, October 18th, the day following the funeral was the due day.

Her dining room table and chairs would go, but Gloria's dressing table and bench was hers. The sofa, easy chair, end table, living room carpet, floor model radio and lamps would be gone. So too would the brass bed and its springs and mattress be taken along with Mark's youth bed. But all cooking and eating items belonged as did all linen and cloth wares, and pillows. Maggie's crib had been a gift and would stay. And folding beds would be kept from the unused spare rooms. There were also a couple of card tables and some folding chairs in the basement which could be put to use. Many people in those days might have considered such furnishings to put them in the lap of luxury, but the young mother was also facing a total eviction deadline of Saturday October 30th.

Gloria Brown faced the worst of all dwellers in what had been Granny's Lodging for after the girl's supposed marriage, agreement between the Millers and Jacob and Burly (who ended up freely doing repairs and janitorial service without pay) were offered to the presumed newly-weds at no cost and at a very minimum for the double room. All the other tenants had paid in advance for the rest of the year and among Granny's records were carbon copies of all payments but the new "treasurer" had never advanced the money to the proper accounts and all of it had been carried away when he disappeared.

But the Sheriff and Mayor quickly learned of the embezzling when the back log of mail was sorted. The word went directly to the Federal District Judge Nehemiah Stillwell. Even before the funeral the top officials of the ten banks which had contrary to regulations loaned out excessive amounts of the deposits of their customers all had received court orders delivered by State Police Officers that the day after the burial of Esther Sue Brown all of the bank officials would appear before the Judge under penalty of extreme fines and possible jail sentences if they failed to come with necessary records.

Judge Stillwell told them that except for Miss Brown from whom no payments had been ever received, all the other apartment dwellers would not be evicted before the end of the year. And as a penalty their stay would be extended to the end of January and also the cost of the moving vans would be paid by the group of banks. All cost which had been covered in the original leases would also be paid. Thus heat, electricity, gas for the ranges, and hot and cold water would all continue as before. And as an add-on the custodial work would also grant Burly Dodge free lodging. The bankers were very unhappy but the Judge also told them that if he had any complaints; he personally was acquainted with J. Edgar Hoover and it would be very easy to get Federal Bank Examiners to come in for full inspections.

A very somber group gathered around what had been the grand lady's table and had cups of warmed up stale coffee and looked through some of the old picture albums. The O'Connors had graciously taken the children into their apartment to just give them some extra loving attention. This left Gloria, the Dahlgrens, Burly, and Garth looking at pictures and reminiscing over good times that would not be forgotten. A little before five the phone rang in the lobby and Garth signaled that he would answer.

"Hello. We're not ready for phone conversation now but I can jot down any message and pass it along. To whom do you wish to speak?"

A well-modulated woman's voice said, "It's urgent that I see Miss Brown and the children as quickly as possible."

"It can't be today. Call again tomorrow."

Her voice became insistent to the edge of bossiness. "Right now is the proper time. I insist she come to the phone. This is very important."

His tones become less gentle as he replied, "Anybody can dial this number and demand things, but while I'm here don't expect to give orders to any of us. Just who do you think you are?"

"I'm Miss Worthington and I am an employee of the State Protective Agency for Children. There must be a good reason I can't speak to Miss Brown. If she's sick I can certainly understand. I'm sorry if I'm too pushy but my employer does expect fast results."

Garth paused. He never liked to be too brusque with others especially if they were being pushed by inconsiderate bosses. He cleared his throat and said, "And I am sorry if I sounded angry. I'm not. I'm one of the friends of the lady you mentioned and it's only been a short time since the funeral of her Grandmother was finished. She's really not able now. Could you call again tomorrow?"

The caller paused to get her breath and said finally, "I'm really supposed to see her and the children as soon as possible. Would it be possible to come by tomorrow at four? And please offer her my sympathy. I didn't know."

"I'm gonna stick my neck out and say that time should work. But tell me your number just in case there's an emergency. Unexpected things often happen."

"You're right. Unless I hear otherwise, expect me at four."

Garth told the others about the woman who had called and offered Gloria the condolence that had been offered. He explained that whenever there is a death in a family there is always a possibility of hazard to little ones so it probably was a good idea to make sure children are okay.

A couple of platters of small sandwiches had been sent over and so there was nibble food for all before bedtime although not much appetite. The children seemed to be holding up quite well but often delayed reactions are worse.

Before Garth went up to his room he realized he had many mixed emotions and the call from Miss Worthington had started some uneasy thoughts. Thus he called James Stillwell to get what information he could about the State Protective Agency for Children. He ended up going over to see James and came back with some information he did not like.

CHAPTER SIX

In many ways Thursday, October 14th, 1937, was just about the worst day of Gloria Brown's life. Everywhere she looked she was haunted by memories and although most of them were good scenes they all were filled with images of the woman who had cared for her ever since her birth. And even though the fake husband and his cohort were responsible for failure to pay for the loan which had been taken to furnish her apartment, she was also filled with fond memories of how well she and the children had lived there.

Thus in the morning when Clancy, Burly, and Garth moved all the things out of her apartment and parked them in the front lobby to ease the job of the crew from the furniture warehouse to carry the repossessed things to their curbside parked truck, she did not really wish to watch it all happen. She was very cordial and kind to the movers, even to the extent of offering them some refrigerated fruit punch left over from the funeral luncheon and thanking them for how carefully they handled everything so that new owners of the used things might not be disappointed.

She even went extra far to thank the three men who had worked diligently to make it easier for the movers. Then one by one she had given them each soft hugs to show her appreciation for all they were all willing to do for her. This was especially so after they moved in two single beds from the vacant upstairs rooms, two folding tables and six folding chairs from the basement, and the rather tattered sofa from what had been Granny's apartment. It was topped off by a couple of floor lamps and the little radio from the double room above.

But by mid-morning when the furniture truck came, any stoic-appearance had vanished and she was on the verge of collapsing. She still had a strong abiding faith in her Savior but it seemed to her there was more darkness than light. She had no idea, not even a hint of what she should do. But words often repeated by her Granny were that when everything starts to be in deep shadows, we must lift our eyes to our Shepherd who is the light of the world.

She remembered countless times when she had sought to be with her grandmother and more often than not had found her praying softly but audibly in her bedroom, quite often kneeling by her bed. Granny's room had often seemed like a chapel where God felt very near.

Gloria quietly wheeled her chair in and bowed her head and besought the Heavenly Father to calm her troubled soul. It is not an infrequent occurrence in places of public worship for some to lift up their arms, palms upward symbolizing that the one praying along silently expected God to give to them whatever was best that day.

As the young mother began to silently beseech God to give her whatever he saw as best she outstretched her arms with palms turned up. And then she became conscious of a soft rustling of cloth behind her and two women moved close and laid gentle hands on her head and shoulders. Then two more came in softly on the carpet and held up her arms. There was then a fifth who came up behind her and softly touched her upper head.

There was a time many years ago in the author's life that he accepted the offer of attempting to lead a particular ministry which he had grave misgivings about whether he could possibly do what was hoped for. At a service of the church the Pastor announced the possibilities and asked the man to come forward to kneel where as many as possible of the congregation as could gather around him for what many called the laying on of hands which symbolized the prayer support and cooperation the church expected to give him. He did receive the help and encouragement he needed. He often also thought later about the several who had taken hold of his hands and arms and held them up much like Aaron and Hur had upheld Moses and his rod in defeating the Amalekites.

After Gloria's time of prayer in which she knew for certain many of her sisters in the faith had also been praying, she paused and began to quietly sing the magnificent doxology Praise God From Whom All Blessings Flow. When she finished and opened her eyes, she was alone. The others had slipped quietly away. But Gloria understood what had happened. She never said anything about it but she knew what it all meant and she smiled again in agreement with Granny's view of how important both sexes are in the work of the Lord.

At noon the two retired folks in apartment 1A, Fred and Sandy Van Epps, sought out Gloria and Maggie and also Dharma and Maureen to have lunch with them. Mark was at school and had his food with him. It was an appreciated offer and Gloria did not mention it but suspected Sandy had been one of the unseen angels sent by the Lord to bring cheer and encouragement. She also had an idea that her Pastor's wife may have been the fifth one and she loved all the ladies even more than before.

After the lunchmeat sandwiches and dish of homemade soup, both mothers retired with their daughters for much needed naps. The funeral day had drained the women and their nights of sleep had been fitful. Gloria again thanked God for her girl which in her own eyes made her richer than a millionaire. Maggie and Mom cuddled up together on the rather old and worn couch which had been Granny's and covered with the beautiful quilt.

At a little after three Mark came banging in the house the way boys often do but it didn't waken his sleeping beauty step-sister. However his mother roused instantly and announced that she was going into the abandoned kitchen to use up leftovers and a few of the smaller cans as well as some left over pork roast.

On that day the Marshal had a very light work load and since most of the use of the various firearms in his arsenal was over until the following week, he felt the time could be well used in cleaning and lubricating his own personal weapons. Thus even though Miss Brown was already wheeling around in the kitchen, there was very adequate space for him to spread oil proof covers on a small part of the table. He got started just before three thirty but was interrupted by the phone.

"Would it be a terrible imposition if I arrived early? I could just sit quietly until the Brown family was ready for me. I'm terribly sorry but my driver has to get some office supplies that just arrived at the Office Supplies Market. If we wait for them, I'll be late doing some extra reports I've just learned about. I'm so sorry to add extra stress," said Miss Penelope Worthington.

Garth relayed the request and Gloria insisted that she would speak to the employee whom it seemed was kept under pressure to do everything her boss ordered immediately if not sooner. "I understand perfectly and it's getting pretty nasty out so you'll certainly be welcome to a cup of fresh coffee that's beginning to perk."

A few minutes later Miss Worthington came dashing up the walk to the door for a chilling heavy drizzle had begun and she had no umbrella.   The Marshal had been watching for her and quickly brought her in and assisted her in hanging up her already drenched light weight coat on a hanger near the lobby register where drying took place rapidly. The man immediately noticed how pale she was and her intermittent shivering told of her chill. She took off her hat which had a broad brim that had kept most of the rain off of her long hair, and placed it on the shelf. She took off her gloves and thrust them in her coat pockets and then hung her purse-like brief case on her shoulder and offered her hand to the man as they properly introduced themselves.

Gloria came wheeling in from the kitchen and the woman's extended hand was almost icy. Penelope said, "I should have worn a winter coat because the car the state gave me needs a new heater. But they're very stingy and expect me to pay any repair bills. And as my vision weakened I had to quit driving and I have to pay a little to a couple of neighborhood kids who take turns bringing me where my boss insists I go."

Gloria said, "I insist you come in the kitchen where it's cozier and let me pour a mug of hot coffee. And although it's earlier than I usually get supper ready, if you haven't eaten yet, as soon as the children and the Marshal come to the table, you'll see I've already set a place for you."

"But it's really against proper procedure to accept gifts from people I have to do business with."

Garth interjected, "In my opinion you look weak from insufficient food today. Just what have you eaten?"

About then Mark and Maggie came in the kitchen and stared at the woman all dressed in black save a crisp white blouse. They were also curious about the very thick spectacles she wore which had clipped onto them dark sunglasses. They politely nodded and shook hands as Garth introduced them.

Then the mother put on a stern face such as Granny sometimes used and said, "Ma'am, do you see the badge that man has on? He's not an ordinary cop or a state police officer, he's an agent of the Federal Government, and you had better answer his questions if you know what's good for you."

Penelope realized as she saw the grins that came onto faces, that the people she would be dealing with were folks with friendly attitudes. "I admit I was very careless today. I was out of milk and just had dry corn flakes for breakfast. And at noon I was rushed and only had a cup of tea. And this coffee I've been sipping has really been warming me."

Gloria began pushing dishes over to the woman and said, "There is no way you are leaving here without eating with us. And if there is some obscure law against attempting to commit suicide by not eating, I'm sure the Marshal could put you under arrest." And then she began to giggle as did the children and man who knew she was just joking.

The visitor joined in the fun a bit by dishing food on her plate and announcing she'd prefer not to be arrested. She then ate quite heartily after all five paused as the children recited grace together. And after the meal was finished Penelope began clearing the table so as to help with washing the dishes. She also heartily thanked her benefactors and proclaimed how much better she felt and also accepted a refill of her coffee mug. She was also aware of how the law man completed his pistol cleaning and oiling task. This did make her nervous.

As soon as the kitchen work was complete he said, "Gloria, I would like a few minutes for a private conversation with Miss Worthington. Would you mind keeping the children in your apartment a while as this lady and I chat about a few things? Is that okay with you ma'am?"

As the trio retreated he asked the visitor if it would make any difference to her if he holstered his 9 mm. Luger and hung it all on his belt. He told her about the beautifully chromed semi-automatic which was his personal property. "When I was a cop in Chicago before Prohibition was repealed, a cousin of mine who is a magnificent gunsmith received this gun from a survivor of The Big War who had gotten it from a German Officer prisoner. My cousin very much altered it by making a new barrel for it which is about three inches longer than normal. He also lengthened the pistol grip and made special magazines which hold twelve rounds each. He also had it chromed. He gave it to me when I was accepted as a Marshal. I am going to load a magazine into it but the safety is on and there will never be a round in the chamber when I am carrying it so I must deliberately crank a shot into the chamber and also release the safety before it can be shot. And I wish to add that it has deadly accuracy over 100 yards which is the length of a football field. Are you okay about my carrying it on my person whenever I am on active duty?"

She nodded her compliance and the man immediately requested that he be shown whatever documents were due to go to Gloria. He scanned the three official papers and after doing so said, "I am going to show you my I.D. card and I wish to see yours. But first tell me how much job training you were given when you were employed and how long have you been employed?"

He was surprised that her only training was only a couple of weeks of working with the lady who had given notice and left the position for Penelope. He told her he had worked with other Marshals for about six months and during that time had to take several night courses to give him a proper understanding of the laws he was sworn to uphold. He also learned she had worked for the agency for only a bit more than two years. She also confided that prior to that she had worked in grocery stores as she attained a state certificate to teach lower grade children as a substitute but her present position although it did not pay better at least gave her a steady salary.

"I spent several hours with an attorney last night into the wee hours. As I looked over these documents, I noticed three items which if you had carried out per your orders might possibly require criminal law being used against you and/or legal suits brought against you from whom your boss would very likely weasel out and let you be the scapegoat. I have encountered several politicians of this ilk."

They were seated across the kitchen table and the young woman began to sniffle and carefully removed her sunglasses and spectacles and wiped around her eyes. He was quite sure it was more tears from fear than eye irritation bothering her and he asked her if the light was too bright and turned off one of the ceiling lights to remove the glare.

She regained her composure and thanked him for the reduced glare and then asked, "Have I done anything wrong? I know our state laws demand a woman be 21 and must give legally acceptable care which means enough income if they aren't married and have an illegitimate child. And I was informed that Hester Sue was the legal guardian of the boy. So my boss told me both the children had to be taken from Miss Brown. But I talked to the Sheriff and he said she had never been legally married and fraudulent documents had been used. I was in a quandary. Even if that sweet lady had been tricked, I couldn't see why she should have her little girl taken. It's different with the boy. His guardian died. I hope you can show me what's right and wrong."

"I'm sure I can help you. You have been told to do three things which violate both State and Federal Law. The first violation would be for you to be the agent to give her the state court injunction that she had to appear for a hearing. State Law requires that only licensed process servers can deliver such orders and you are not licensed. The other possibility is that a Judge can issue a warrant demanding presence in court and this is carried out by a law officer who arrests the person who might be a felon.

"The second thing you were expected to do was to enter their living quarters so that you could ascertain if they meet minimum standards and also if food and clothing etcetera were adequate and proper. Normally only an officer of the law or a person such as a health or safety inspector could enter but there are Federal and State mandates that a search warrant is necessary except under extraordinary situations such as police pursuing a robber or escapee. But if a mother willingly invites an inspector, there would be no need for a warrant.

"The third situation which is the most serious is when the inspector, without written permission of the mother, attempts to remove a child or children from the premises without a specific court order to do so. So hypothetically if you escorted Mark or Margaret out the door to supposedly show them the orphanage and possibly even let them think they will be detained there, you could possibly be placed under arrest and charged with attempted kidnapping.

"I am sure you are well aware of the kidnapping of the Lindbergh child in 1932 which led to a severe addition to Federal Law which supersedes all state laws. The kidnapping law carries a possible death penalty under certain circumstances. Kidnapping could even be a very grave offense for any person who even promotes it. So this third set of your instructions which is admittedly vague enough to be misunderstood could be a deliberate attempt to cause trouble for you. I intend to look into the matter because there is no doubt in my mind that you are an innocent bystander. Please don't be afraid. I mean you no harm. I didn't intend to frighten you. But I would like to know how your instructions came into your thoughts after you read all the fine print on these papers."

He seated her in the lobby in one of the easy chairs and waited until she began to regain her composure. She admitted, "I couldn't make out much of the fine print because I dropped my magnifying glass this morning and it shattered. I probably should have asked a neighbor to read them to me. My eyes are getting very weak. I had to quit driving a few months ago because several times I almost caused accidents and now I have to pay a couple of young folks to drive me around. And that old car is a 1925 Chrysler but it really burns a lot of gas and I wish they'd given me one that wasn't so worn out. And I have to turn in the bills to keep it going and they're so slow to reimburse me. Oh! I'm sorry I keep rattling off."

He chuckled and replied, "I get nervous and rattle on too. But before we go on I'm sure Gloria would like a chance to explain at least part of her problem and how two lying con men tricked a lot of people. The one who tricked her and everyone around her with fraudulent wedding documents is now in Joliet Prison. Learn her side before you jump to conclusions. And I also want Doctor Williams to take a look at your eyes. His room is down the hall from mine and he should be back shortly. Okay? Gloria's apartment is right this way and for now I'll take the kids to the kitchen table to fool around."

As the trio were each drawing silly pictures and playing "guess what it is," the lobby phone rang and Garth got up to answer it. Penny's driver said, "I'm Connie Borgman and her car quit dead after I pulled in her driveway. I didn't do anything bad so I think I owe her some money back cuz she paid me at the start. And it's her birthday on Saturday, October 16th, so wish her a happy birthday for me."

"I will certainly see we all wish her the best. And don't be worrying that you did anything wrong. She already told me the car was almost worn out and not dependable and someone here will see to it she has a safe ride home in a car with a good heater. I'll let her know you did fine."

After a few more minutes of giggling time in the kitchen, the Dr. arrived and was quickly told of the visitor's vision problem and agreed to at least give the lady a quick optical check. He told her, "It's very serious, but it is a matter which can be taken care of and an almost normal vision be restored. I'm not skilled in any way for the treatment needed to remove cataracts but currently one of the top surgeons in this country is teaching prospective eye doctors at the medical school which is part of the college in Crawford."

The woman was almost too scared to respond. She was certain she'd be legally blind in just a few months. The Dr. said, "At the very least you should let Dr. Isaac Echenstein examine your eyes and if necessary set up whatever treatment is best for you. I have his number while he's at the medical school. And I am certain a ride can be provided for you."

For the first time in many months Miss Worthington had a smidgen of hope that she might have a chance to delay the ominous blackness which she had been sure was inevitable. And as soon as an appointment with the eye surgeon had been penciled in, it so happened that Burly Dodge came in to get cleaned up so he could go out for supper. The tall slim lady in black caught his eye and he dashed into the lobby restroom to wash his oily hands so the Marshal could introduce him. She rather shyly shook hands with the large man who was a bit taller than her but almost twice as wide. And both of them could hardly speak. Her sight of him was blurred but she felt that between the three men she was suddenly very safe and hopeful. And her brief encounter with the young mother had given her a strong conviction that separating her from the children would be cruel and perhaps even criminal.

Burly rushed through a quick change out of work coveralls and into presentable casual ware. During these moments Garth was trying to get through to State Representative Malcolm Loocerson to inform the man who happened to be the chairman of the board of the State Protective Agency for Children that it was absolutely essential that Miss Worthington be granted one of the sick days spelled out in her employment contract.

"And you need to have your accounting office prepare to remit to her the balance she was never paid for car repairs the state is responsible for. There is also the question of severance pay should she give you notice and also she was never given her vacation pay or allowed to take time off. If you use any pressure tactics to get her compliance to your ambiguous orders, as a Federal Marshal I do have an open contact with the F.B.I. So be very careful what you do. And, umm, have a nice day."

Burly very shyly approached the slim lady in black and said, "I heard that your Chrysler is almost ready for the junk yard. My Buick is in really good working order and I wanted to go to the parts store to get a can of brake fluid and some anti-freeze and that's down the street from your office so it wouldn't be a bit of a bother to give you a ride. But after that I was gonna go down to the gas station and fill up my tank and then to the lunch room where they make super desserts and chili so I kin have a little supper and if you didn't have any milk today it would be really good for you to maybe have a cup of cocoa and a donut with me. Anyhow I really hate to eat alone. Food seems to taste better when you have someone pleasant to chat with. Don't you think so?"

She rode along with him and enjoyed the warm comfort of the heater as he made his first two stops. A polite and very gentle man like Burly was a unique and pleasant safe experience for her. It had actually been only when she was still in high school that fellows had shown her any interest and she had quickly perceived that most of them only desired some kind of affair with the tallest girl in school.

He never even touched her unless it was to clasp her hand to steady her as she entered or left his auto. She enjoyed the cocoa and donut but was a little stubborn about paying for her share with change out of her purse. He was even more stubborn about how he was an old-fashioned man who would be insulted if he couldn't pay when she was his guest. She had not for years experienced such gallantry.

Early on Friday morning a Process Server approached Gloria before Garth could bring his car around to bring the lady and her wheelchair back to the hospital. By then she was able to limp smoothly around using a cane but would require the removal of the cast to be replaced by a stretch band on her leg. Even if the Marshal was convinced the service of a summons was incorrect, he did not dare to interfere. And so Gloria could not refuse to face a judge and review board which would be meeting on the 13th of November.

A couple of hours before the process serving, Burly and Miss Worthington were on the way to the Medical School of the college where she would be meeting with Dr. Echenstein for a thorough eye examination. It only took a little more than an hour for the drive but there were papers she had to fill out. By then she had been coaxed into calling the man Burly and she had retaliated that she preferred her first given name in personal conversations.

Burly's very serious answer had been for him a very sudden change from his usual very polite chatter. He had suddenly said, "I really want to say Penny instead of Penelope. I think you're much prettier than even freshly minted pennies. I hope you don't think I'm too fresh but that's what I thought since the first second I saw you. Oh Golly! Hoof and mouth disease! Open mouth and insert foot."

He turned away from her in embarrassment and she was silent for a moment in unbelief before she said, "If my vision was even a tiny fraction as good as yours, it's possible I might think of you as a handsome man. Since I was a little girl, I've hardly ever had any compliments like yours. And the only use of school mates with Penny as a name was when they used my family name and said I must be worth a ton of pennies. And it was meant as a taunt, not praise."

She expected the Dr. who had such experience to be an old man but was shocked that he didn't seem much more than middle age. And his smile and immediate friendship to both of them made her feel right at home. She had filled out the papers given to her and then he told her his appreciation that she had followed his instructions to avoid solid foods for breakfast. "By your avoidance of greasy or solid food and just using beverage and juice, you avoid any possible upset of your digestive systems which sometimes causes nausea or vomiting when it is necessary for me to put you under anesthesia. But after the visit I'm sure this gentleman will not deny you a chance to eat a hearty breakfast to restore your strength after the ordeal I put you through." And then they all had a soft laugh.

It was approaching noon before the lady was over any wooziness and the kindly Dr. had a chance to allay her fears. "If you had not come to me or one of my good colleagues, before next year was over, nothing could be done for you. But as it is right now you could hardly have come at a better time. You have growing cataracts on both eyes and this is a very good time to remove them. I am strongly recommending it be taken care of now. And I often think the Good Lord has more to do with my schedule than I do for I have Monday morning wide open and if you permit me I can set it up to be done at the Nightingale Hospital which would be much more convenient for you. And I would bring along a few of my best students, not to assist yet, but to observe and learn."

Penny said quietly, "I don't know how I could ever repay you for I have almost nothing in the bank."

"Kind lady, I get good compensation from the college for my teaching and I have written a number of medical books from which I still get royalties. I'm not rich but I am comfortably well off. Also state employees will also get a small part of their bills taken care of. And if necessary there can be small loans. So please do not fret over the least important matter. The important matter is having your vision brought back at least close to normal. Well, shall I set it up?"

It was set up that the following Monday would be the start of a four day stint in the hospital but that it would be necessary that she had food and lodging taken care of in a private residence and that an additional seven day stay would probably be more than sufficient for completion of the healing process which would then be followed by testing for new glasses.

After the late bountiful breakfast was before them and the blessing asked, she was able to dig in but was very silent. She had so many things to mull over and she had no idea how she could repay Burly for all the car expense and then the huge pile of waffles and sausage he had paid for. And he had told her he wanted a day off from his two janitorial jobs so she needed not to worry. He told her that he was sure she might be very surprised at how God often sent things to his children that they never really expected.

Burly had her back to her office/quarters about an hour before the customary closing time and Penny was not really required to use part of a sick day to work, but she was very conscientious and insisted she finish her shift. Connie had brought in all the cartons from the store and then re-locked the door and slid her spare car and office keys into the mail slot on the door. The man helped the lady to put all the supplies in their proper places and then extracted a promise that she would lock up promptly at noon and come with him with mysterious hints that she come with him regarding birthday considerations. She had already told him it would be her 35th anniversary, but hadn't revealed her age until he told her he was going to be 45 on November 30th.

At ten forty five on Saturday a young man came dashing up to the office with an urgent delivery for Miss Worthington from State Representative Malcolm Loocerson. In brief it was an apology for what he had just supposedly had learned about sloppy record keeping which was responsible for what almost looked like embezzlement. Within was a complete record of all payments made to her and a separate record of all shortfalls to her in vacation days, sick days, and automobile expenses including cost for drivers. The check took her breath away. And when Burly picked her up he was very glad to get her to the bank which was open from ten till two on Saturdays.

Burly told Penny, "Garth told me he had a talk with Loocerson and this was followed up by a second talk from F.B.I. Agent Smith. Both cautioned the man to be sure he had accurate records and proof of proper payment. Garth and I both think that the Agency is making some significant money from adoption fees paid by affluent prospective parents and also by some manipulating of fees paid to state picked foster parents. I saw a high school play of Hamlet and there was a line something like there was something rotten in the state of Denmark.

"Dear lady, since you have a bit of a nest egg, and since I am sure you will regain most of your sight, it might be wise to make a clean cut with the Agency. I'm sure you could do pretty good even as a substitute teacher and I'm not flush but I have been tucking away a bit and I could give you a loan if it became necessary."

She was silent for a long moment on their way to what had been Granny's Lodging before speaking very quietly. "Burly, I've only known you a couple of days but I trust you implicitly. Only the Lord could be a better friend than you. But I could never borrow from you nor can I imagine ever being able to pay you pack for what you've already been doing for me. I can hardly wait to have enough vision to see you clearly."

At the Lodging she had mixed emotions when there were no people or voices. The man very carefully led her down to the very dimly lit basement where Mark's party had taken place. She was led into the dark main room and dim lights were turned on behind her and a large group of folks suddenly called out a happy birthday. Festoons had been strung such as Mark had seen and she was seated at the long plywood on sawhorse table but with a long oilcloth on it.

All of the people Penny had met on the previous day were there as well as Dharma, Maureen, the retired VanEpps, Erica Pulaski, and Heidi Dahlgren. A large three layer, beautifully decorated birthday cake with Penny written on it, but no candles, and no confession of who baked it was the centerpiece. Fruit punch and scoops of ice cream were served all around after the birthday song was sung.

Penelope declared that she wished all would call her Penny and also almost tearfully thanked all for her last birthday celebration had been when she had been fifteen and since then no one had made such gestures of kindness. Even at her church it was only the youngsters who ever had a fuss made over them.

Then she received little gifts such as hankies or small scarves from total strangers. But Erica gave her a coupon good for a shampoo, haircut, and gently curved permanent. Heidi gave her a ticket good for a 50% discount at a woman's clothing shop and also offered her a seldom-used dress of her own which had mistakenly been picked for her for Christmas at a store in Chicago by an aunt who thought her niece was taller. But Heidi also gave Penny some lingerie which had perhaps been used once and then washed so it smelled and felt new.

Burly stoically drove Gloria, Heidi, and Penny to the dress store but pled with the ladies to get her into a bright dress which wouldn't look like mourners black. He had added that they ought to get her a hat which looked feminine instead of witch ware. And then he took them all to get bowls of chili but denied them donuts or pastries because of the birthday cake they had each had.

The following morning Burly picked Penny up in plenty of time to arrive at the Full Gospel Chapel before the service. They were politely greeted but many of the attendees seemed puzzled at who she was. And Mr. Dodge noticed that almost every person wore black or very dark colors and all the women wore hats much like the bonnets pioneer women used to wear but these were all in very subdued colors. All the men had on dark suits like his which he usually reserved for very solemn times such as funerals. He kept a straight face but the congregation very much resembled a picture he had seen in an old history book of a convention of Salem witches. But the witches had seemed much happier.

Even with the sharp glances at Penny, she was not perturbed for she could not focus on them. She had been able to tell to a degree that her beautiful blue dress with a counterpoint of gorgeous flowers would attract much notice and probably invite phone calls and many visits to warn her of such ungodliness.

Burly asked the usher if there was a booklet or pamphlet which would tell him more about their customs and practices. The attractive printout had on its cover the name of the church and a simple but meaningful motto, No Creed but Christ; No Law but Love. And then the Pastor came over and told about some of the outreach of the congregation.

"We have a food pantry and have regular drives to replenish it. We also have a used clothing ministry where people who are desperate can be helped. And we offer various counseling sessions. It's our goal to bring people to Jesus and then by our practice, which our booklet explains, bring them into a life which eliminates worldliness and ungodly habits."

The big man quickly noticed the sharp stares Penny received and he could sense she was becoming very uncomfortable in a place which should bring comfort. He promised the clergyman he would attentively read their literature and then quickly took Penny to her quarters. They were both silent about the service. It was true that the essential message had been given but there had seemed to what some called a "holier than thou" chip on their shoulders. He offered to take her out for dinner but she insisted there was a simple casserole awaiting them. It was not quite ready yet, so he carefully read through their anti-worldliness doctrine.

After eating and washing the dishes, they sat sipping coffee as he began to unburden himself regarding her church's book of rules. "I've been thinking about flowers. Have you ever considered how many different kinds there are and how many different colors? And what about birds? They are every color of the rainbow and more. If God thinks colors are worldly or ungodly, why didn't he make everything black or gray? Or did he invent all the colors and made eyes so that colors can usually be seen? Sometimes writers think they are so smart that God must be stupid.

"And then try to figure how many different flavors and varieties of food God invented in the first place. Should a book be telling you that buying or eating certain foods are sinful habits? And how about the Sabbath? Jesus said it was made for us and for our good. We weren't made for it. The old Pharisees figured they knew so much about what people could do or not do that they came up with over six hundred rules. They must have thought God was stupid if he thought ten were enough. And Jesus summed it all up in just two. Love God and obey him and love your neighbor and help him. I want to follow Jesus' plan. Don't you?

"I know any church has to have some rules so things can be done decently and in order. And I think neither one of us want churches to be run by Pharisees with more rules than anyone can remember. But I also know there are a lot of churches that want people to put Jesus first and anyone else second. And I would be very glad if you would let me take you to visit one of the Nazarene churches like the Baptist minister mentioned at Granny's funeral. Would you go with me tonight? And would you wear this pretty dress again?"

Penny quickly agreed to going to the Nazarene service and as quickly began to inwardly agree that in spite of her long time association with the Full Gospel Chapel and great empathy with most of what it did, at heart there were indeed things which seemed amiss; seemed at least somewhat off center with the full purpose of its Master. Her fellow members seemed almost alien to what her heart and

Burly's convictions were. And in strange parallel matters her clothing and even the feel of her hair since Erica's ministrations seemed much more correct.

The entire uplifting and joyful atmosphere at the evening service at the Crawford Nazarene Church took hold of Penny and she felt as if she belonged there. Chester Lemunyon, the pastor, was upbeat and hardly able to restrain expressing his joy and delight in the Lord. His preaching was lovingly forceful and every part of the service was magnetism drawing folks closer to the Lord. The service concluded with an open invitation to a coffee and cookie fellowship. Then the pastor and his wife Effie joined the two visitors in a laughter filled conversation which gave much info about the Good Shepherd Shelter. Penny came home with a completely different view of how orphan and mother programs ought to be in which a major thrust must be training in the fear of the Lord and trust in the Savior.

With time to spare Burly was able to get Penny to the receiving desk at the hospital to sign in and could be wheeled to her room. He promised to stop in to see her that afternoon when the operations were complete and she was able to have visitors. Just as he was leaving, Erica came rushing in to confer with the financial officer. She had received just that morning from her auto insurance agent a very welcome check which she had not expected to ever see. She had not even heard that the Buick she had leased to Jacob Ebner had been found burnt and bullet riddled near the Okeefenokee swamp and all evidence by the police and F.B.I. concluded it had been stolen and burned by an arsonist. Thus her upright agent had rushed a fair settlement to her.

Erica's entire spread out clan was basically Roman Catholic but a great number of the wide spread Pulaski family all had many good Protestant friends and acquaintances. It had an open philosophy that God the Father had vast numbers of children in the great diversity of Christianity. Thus when folks other than Catholic were doing Jesus' work on earth, it was only proper that a good Catholic would (without depriving their own parishes) lend help.

Therefore as soon as Erica regained the money she had been sure was lost and gone forever, she immediately fixed her thoughts on lessening the burdens of others. Very quickly any due hospital payments were made on behalf of Granny and Gloria. She also guaranteed that Penelope's bill and the cost of new glasses would be taken care of. But she went beyond this and promised that after Miss Worthington was allowed to leave the hospital in four or five days, she herself would underwrite the cost of quiet rest and insist the young lady must stay in her home for the seven or eight days of recuperation and that Clara Pulaski, one of her nieces who worked as a hospital bookkeeper, would be available for the little extra attention required.

Erica was also aware of the impending basement sale which would begin that evening of all things that would not be left behind when the banks foreclose. By the Judge's decree no one except Gloria and the two children were forced to be gone by Sunday, October 31st, but without any exception all the rest had been choosing to move out then and would receive the balances due to them and also the cost of moving. She informed Gloria that the big basement of her home was dry and safe and virtually empty so that it could serve for cost free storage of essentials. She did not say so but she held in reserve whatever an apartment might cost the young mother for a month or so until she could acquire a job.

Finally she also laid aside enough to help her grandson purchase a truck perhaps a year newer, but this was also secret. Then she sent a generous donation to the Good Shepherd Shelter after her Priest commended that work and its motto that no child should be neglected or abused.

Garth was inwardly by Sunday evening steaming over the Child Protective Agency philosophy that in almost any case it had to be the woman who was to blame. And yet there had hardly been a case where a man was ever really found to be the guilty party. He yearned to do something to prevent what he considered the crime of taking children away from a good mother when scheming men were the guilty ones and an all-male legislature had put legal restrictions on females under twenty one against seeking redress in court or even to own property.

He went to see the friendly attorney James Stillwell and there was literally nothing he could do. He could not be a legal guardian to Mark because he was neither a married man nor a blood relative. The same applied to Maggie. He ended up calling his boss, Major Stillwell and what he learned gave him a faint gleam of light.

He approached Gloria after Penny was safely in the recovery room and asked, "Have you ever had an airplane ride?" "No. And I don't think I would want to." "I haven't either and I remember an uncle who told me the only way he wanted to fly was if he could keep one foot on the ground." She chuckled and replied, "I don't think you'd get too high."

"Gloria, I'm not trying to make a joke, but if you will go with me tomorrow, I am going to have a very serious talk with two very important people regarding a long term job assignment and there is a possibility it might somehow become possible that there might be a chance of a job for you without separation from your kids.

"Fred and Sandy VanEpps would be willing to tend the store and Heidi said she could help too. The street has plenty of parking and it's no strain to go through the back basement door to do your shopping downstairs. I have no guarantee but who knows what gates the Lord can swing open for you? And you will have a nice dinner, too. Take a chance. Who knows what might come of it?"

Chapter Seven

Marshal Stone did not need much persuasion to get Miss Brown to agree to trust him enough to spend most of Tuesday with him and also to dare to go for an airplane ride with him. She did not have to think twice when he assured her that even though there were no guarantees that the issues of her final custody of her loved ones would be all taken care of, he would be doing everything that was legal and moral to help her. Even if she had not already seen continual evidences that his Christianity was a rock which matched the name of Stone, the continuing testimonies about the man from her dear friend Heidi would have been more than sufficient.

As tersely as possible as they drove, he summarized the position in which he found himself regarding assisting Gloria in securing a permanent relationship with the children. "I had thought I might be able to be their guardian and perhaps hire you as a housekeeper or such. But the state regulations make it very clear that I would have to be a blood relation and also if I hired an employee she must be in her own separate living quarters but that would also require you to be 21. The other clinker in the furnace is that I would have to be married for two years or more and there would be strict rules about who actually would have rights such as adoptions bring. I want very much to help preserve your little family. I love both the children and I have great respect for you and how you show them your love."

He was surprised she had never seen Crawford's minor airport. The state's main east-west highway happened to be the dividing line between Stillwell and Crawford and went south at the Eagle river and ended at Southport. But there was a county road about two miles south of Crawford which also connected to Southport. And just south of the center of town was the airport which had a small sector with a tall fence topped with barbed wire. Access from the county road to this military section was only through a gate such as is used at railroad crossings and there was a tiny booth and an armed guard. Access to the field through the surrounding fence could be patrolled. And all the sentries wore M P bands on their sleeves.

There were two hangars within the fence and several other small buildings. An American flag proudly waved in the small yard between the buildings. Just inside the gate which opened to the runway, there stood a very shiny Ford Tri-motor airplane. Painted on both its sides were the normal insignia and emblems which designated it to be a military plane. Also inside that gate were a couple of fuel tanks.

Garth halted at the gate, opened his window, and waved at the guard who smiled and waved back as he picked up a phone and made a quick call to the guard house. In less than a minute another M P hurried over and asked the Marshal for his I.D. and pass which he briefly glanced at and then told the other guard to open the gate and pointed to a parking spot next to the biggest building. "Good morning Marshal, Sir; and you too, Ma'am. The Colonel and Senator are expecting you both in the big hall."

The couple entered the small mess hall and a man in a spotless white uniform with an equally spotless large apron (apparently the Mess Sargent) greeted them at the entry and rather nervously saluted the Marshal who returned the salute although these salutes were not necessary except to actual military officers from those of lesser rank.

They were led down a hallway past the compact kitchen. At the end of the hallway were double doors with mirrors on them presumably for G.I.s to check their appearances before an inspection. A sign above the double door designated that area as Quarters and across the hall from the kitchen a sign above the wide door said it was a Briefing Room. The soldier in white indicated they should enter.

Gloria had got a glimpse of her reflection and was as satisfied as most women would be that her dress was not wrinkled from the long ride or her appearance uncouth. She was wearing what she had worn when she had learned of the protective custody but she had a cheerful kerchief which had been intended to keep her hair captive and she had on a white cardigan sweater lest she be chilled during an airplane ride. She had gloves in her purse and Garth had assisted her in removing her autumn coat and had hung it up in the hall as they had followed the Cook.

A booming voice bid them welcome as they entered and Colonel P. J. Taylor hurried over to shake hands and introduce himself. He wore his dress uniform. His chest was colorful with service bars from places all over the world where he had served and only military personnel could figure out from the bars on his sleeves how very long he'd been in the army. He directed them over to a very distinguished gentleman in clothes which gave the impression he had money for an exquisite wardrobe. Both men were about Garth's height and each had name pins and both men seemed to be upper middle aged and with graying hair but almost youthful faces. The second man was Senator Oscar Silvers from Pennsylvania. Both of them were involved in determining military budgeting. And both of them had very similar viewpoints.

There was an oval table in the middle of the room. There were two very comfortable padded seats at each side and the Senator indicated that the newcomers sit opposite him and the Colonel. He said, "Both of us have seen the police and FBI reports and both of us have total sympathy with you Miss Brown. We are outraged by such a thing even being considered to be done to you. We do not live in the dark ages and such male chauvinism needs to be excised. So we wish you to tell us briefly exactly what happened if you would be so kind."

Gloria gave a quite concise overall picture of what had happened that frightful Thursday and then asked if it would be okay to tell them about the last note from her deceased Grandmother. "She gave me some good advice that would be good for anyone. And I'd like you to hear it." She very briefly gave them a direct quote as to what it meant and closed with the motto, "Never give in and never give up."

Both of the rather imposing gentlemen pondered it and both ended up with smiles on their faces indicating acceptance. The Colonel broke his silence and said to the

Andrew Nelson

Senator, "Oscar, even aside from the theological implications, that's darned good advice. Don't you agree?"

"I certainly do. Let me tell you that I have often grown very weary trying to promote constitutional truth found in the Pledge of Allegiance where it says we expect liberty and justice for all. I mustn't ever surrender to what is wrong or quit promoting what's right. I believe every citizen of this great country regardless of skin color or gender ought to have equal opportunities. We still have great lacks of justice when it comes to education, employment, discrimination, and even wages. No matter what the person's color, origin, or gender there should be fairness. I'm afraid some of the laws passed by various legislatures do fall far short from the wishes of the writers of our Constitution, but I fear that only as these inequities are judged by our Supreme Court will each state be forced to obey our basic law of the land. But in your case, Miss Brown, we are right now not legally able to do much, however there is at least one possibility we all want to consider. How say you, P.J.?"

"In line with your thinking, Oscar, I'd like to comment about military justice. I know there is still much prejudice by service people toward those with different religion or background and skin color is still a problem. But we do have rules that must be followed no matter what any commander has as a personal agenda. We are making headway but it's likely there's always going to be rivalry between the army, navy, and coast guard. But this is a friendly rivalry which ends up as unity when our country is threatened from the outside.

"Possible outside threats to our country are actually the main reasons we came together today. Herr Hitler, with

162

his buddy Mussolini, is clearly desirous to conquer all of Europe and put it under Nazi control. If he ever achieved that it's a certainty that North America would be next. He has already got a huge espionage and sabotage network functioning overseas to weaken his future targets in places like Africa. Our President is kept well informed about this. But this nation's top military leaders have also been paying close attention to what many of us think is a grave danger in the Pacific. Many of us are very concerned about Japan becoming a threat to us. I know there has been much optimism over diplomatic talks we have been having with Japan, but a large portion of our top military leaders are at least nervous about it.

"And now let me show you the connection between our glance at world politics and the reason we met today. And just so Miss Brown will not be concerned over whether military secrets will be discussed; what we will be offering is a plan which may shortly be approved and be revealed to the press for public consumption. The only part not fully agreed is the Federal budget which will be required and is an important issue which Oscar and I will be fitting into the overall figures for total military expenditures."

He got up and went over to the end wall of the room which had a full-size cork board onto which documents, maps, and blueprints could be secured. A large drape which covered the board could be readily pulled to the side to reveal the covered contents. He signaled the others to slide their chairs away from the table and to place them in a row in front of the display. He drew the drape enough to the side to reveal a map about four times the size of motorist's road maps. But it mainly showed Eagle Island, the river in which it stood in the middle and the opposite shores of the river and roads.

He used a lecturer's pointer to indicate the predominantly Amerindian populated Ottawa Village near the middle of the island and the Stone house just south of it. He explained that the large map had been put together from plane photos taken of everything. And on the southern tip of the island where both branches of the river joined together were some bright red lines showing where a training camp was to be started.

The Colonel then moved the drape fully open to show a greatly enlarged map of the red lined section. He said. "Both of these maps were prepared from aerial photos. The red section on the larger map shows a probable location of the main construction which hopefully will be completed by the end of June for a facility which is tentatively going to be named Eagle Camp. There will be a dock and boat ramp and a boat storage building for winter use. There will be several Quonset type buildings of various sizes for quarters, kitchen and mess hall, repair shops, a few cottages for families of permanent staff, a few small storage buildings and also an adequate rifle and pistol range. There is also to be a small horse stable."

The Senator stood and said, "I'll take a turn now and give a bit of explanation why Eagle Camp should be necessary. It is going to be training young men to be counterparts for conservation agents who oversee enforcement of hunting and fishing laws and also could be backups for border patrols and guards at places for entry or exit of our borders. But at the camp there would also be extensive training in wilderness survival, use of horses, and extreme training in effective use of firearms and marksmanship, as well as some of the skills needed by law enforcement people in handling felons or troublemakers. This entire training program would require 6 months. We are hoping there can be a dozen graduates every six months. And what we have mentioned about Hitler and Japan could become major worries for our nation's security as time goes by. The permanent staff would include a First Sargent or Lieutenant, a Mess Sargent, and a couple of people with maintenance skills."

He cleared his throat and continued, "Major Colfax, the Marshal's superior officer, has chosen this young man to be in charge of the camp and give them all their major training. He has not yet given answer as to whether he will accept this great responsibility and that is a big part of the reason we met here today. But as the old saying goes, what really put burrs under our saddles is the state's unfeeling treatment of an innocent woman. If improper rules can cause such heartache to one of our citizens, the same twisted logic can be used to hurt any citizen. Oh! The cook is peeking in the door. It must be time for lunch."

As they rose from their seats and made for the door, Garth spoke quietly to Gloria, "I haven't given my final word to my superior but there are still a few considerations that may have a bearing on what I really ought to do. But anything I decide still revolves around whether or not I'll be able to help you in your crisis."

The cook pointed out a small buffet with a fruit basket, things needed for a good tossed salad, trays of crackers and cheese, and an assortment of cookies for dessert. Carafes of coffee and tea as well as pitchers of juice were on the table at which they would be eating. The man in white explained,

"It's all light food lest any might have upset stomachs with heavy food, especially if anyone is not used to flying and could get nauseous."

As they all nibbled their tasty food the Colonel said, "My coworker had government business to conduct in Chicago for a couple of days and I ordered our plane to bring him here. We'll be taking off at about 1:30 which will give us an afternoon sun as we fly around Eagle Island. When the noon sun is right above us it's harder to see things than when there is more shadow. So we're not rushed and there is an assortment of nibble things such as peanuts and also a cooler of assorted pop aboard ship as desired."

When it was about time to board the plane, back in Stillwell Burly was visiting Penny. He had a little bouquet of fragrant flowers in a vase to give her. It would be a couple more days before she would have some light admitted to her eyes, but the man said she could at least smell the wee gift he brought her. It was safely on the dresser when he went to her to gently shake her hand and she was very reluctant to release her two-handed grip on his big hand.

She quietly offered her thanks and then added, "I can't tell you how impatient I am to see your face. In my mind I picture you as the best friend I've ever had. No other person I've gotten acquainted with has ever been so gentle and kind and encouraging to me. Oh my goodness! Jesus knows I'm not trying to put him second. You and I both know what the motto says that if he isn't Lord of all, he isn't Lord at all. But in my heart you're as close to second as anyone I've ever known."

"Golly, Penny. I can't hardly remember what I was gonna say. Uh! Well! I just have to say even with half your face covered with bandages and stuff; to me you're still pretty as a new penny."

Back at the airport the Captain who was pilot came in and said to Miss Brown, "Before we go aboard I'd like to tell you about the Ford Tri-motor. It's currently bragged up as being the strongest airplane made for there is only metal instead of canvas used on the wings and controls. It is extremely durable and with three engines instead of one or two very capable of adequate power for all flying circumstances. Any questions?"

Gloria rather timidly said, "Amelia Earhart used to tell how safe airplanes were and even a woman could learn to fly one. But in July her two engine plane disappeared in the middle of the ocean and they never found it or her or the man who was helping on the plane. And if that could happen to a lady everybody thought was one of the best pilots, is it safe for me even in the kind of plane the newspapers call a Tin Goose?"

Senator Silvers helped the young lady slip into her coat and then patted her encouragingly on her shoulder before saying, "Let me answer. I'm no pilot but I do know we won't be running out of gas on our jaunt which was a certain cause of Amelia's disappearance. Nor will we be crossing any big bodies of water. But in a great emergency we could land in one of the pastures or on a highway which is just the same as a runway. And we're not going over the Rocky Mountains. So I do not want you to fear. Okay?"

The Colonel then led them to the Ford Tri-motor and pointed out the Lieutenant who was the Co-pilot and also two non-coms who were wore side arms but were both to be taking photos. "Miss Brown, the Senator and I request that you and the Marshal allow your pictures to be taken with us beside the plane which has the nickname you used of The Tin Goose. Each of us will be given copies later."

There were pairs of seats down the center and Garth and Gloria were placed in the front most where they could observe the actions of the pilot and co-pilot. The two soldiers were assigned the rearmost seats and the Senator and Colonel sat behind the young pair. Each seat had a set of padded earphones which included a small microphone at one side. The mikes had push button controls so that whatever was spoken could be heard on all earphones. Gloria was told she'd appreciate that she could hear and be heard over the considerable noise from the three engines.

There were rows of windows on each side. The soldiers with cameras already had their instructions on what photos were needed to supplement those earlier taken to prepare the maps which had been shown in the Briefing Room. And of course everybody had to be securely belted in both for the take-off and during the flight.

The pilot spoke to all the passengers before the engines were started. "Please be wearing the earphones. The three engines have a total of more than seven hundred horsepower and while we're on the ground taxiing the sound level is very great. Once we're air borne it will be quieter but still too loud for comfortable conversation. And also please expect some bouncing the way an auto does until our wheels leave the ground. Thank you."

Each of the seats had single armrests on their outer sides and a wider center armrest for two passengers to share. After the engines were all started and the throttles advanced, the plane began its short approach from the side of the main runway. And this was the bumpiest part of the taxiing. But the series of bumps scared Gloria and she tensed up and grasped the ends of the arm rests for all she was worth even though her seat belt safely secured her.

But when the plane was onto the much smoother actual runway and picking up speed until they were climbing away from the ground, the young mother could relax and exhale. And then she realized that she had grabbed Garth's hand and was squeezing it. She quickly released his hand and clasped her hands together on her lap and looked furtively toward him as if what she had done was inappropriate. He gave her a lopsided grin and mouthed, "No problem. It's okay."

Never having been for a plane ride before, the sensation of the take-off briefly disorientated Gloria's nerve reactions for as the wheels lifted off the runway it seemed as if she was on a goofy elevator but very quickly as the altitude increased it seemed to her that she was standing still in space and the world was dropping away from her and going backwards. But what really dazzled her perception was when the plane was leveled off at a couple of thousand feet above ground and all the world below seemed like tiny toy objects. And the amazing view for miles around them was as if everything below was microscopic, yet incredibly beautiful to her eyes.

As Eagle Island was being rapidly approached, their altitude was reduced to a couple of hundred feet above the taller trees and the northern hills for better observation of Ottawa Village and the Stone house. They noticed a crew of men busily re-shingling the bottom four or five feet of the western edge of the gambrel roof. Garth had heard nothing about any accident or damage to the Stone house.

The Colonel clicked on his microphone so all could hear him as the Pilot reduced altitude for a closer look in which many of the workers waved at the plane. "I'm sure this was not even mentioned on the weather reports for there were no deaths or injuries. But reports that my staff bring to me include plenty of details I'd usually rather not hear about. Since we will probably be starting Camp Eagle in the spring and since Mayor Tootoosee, actually Chief and his council will be negotiating with the government regarding part of the Stone house being used for various Village functions, we requested news silence about the mishap.

"Here's what happened. Although statewide weather conditions were close to normal, there was a fluke in an arctic condition which caused the normal winds to funnel along the river which centuries ago apparently had been a gorge. The air flow was midway between hurricane and tornado fierceness. Two large oaks were pushed over and smashed against the roof. The continuing wind tore off shingles on the bottom edge of the roof but also ripped off roof boards leaving a large gap right above the outer wall. And then a squall came and a torrent of water poured onto the wall thoroughly soaking the plaster.

"As soon as I knew what was happening my office issued orders and a platoon of soldiers was on the site within a few hours to assist the village people in any way possible. It was necessary to tear all the soggy plaster and lath down and haul it away but inside work will be needed. This is as much as I know, but I repeat there were no deaths or serious injuries.

"But there is one other thing. The Marshal has relatives up near Mackinaw City, Michigan, who might be candidates to take over the work from which Rudolph and Elisabeth Stone will be retiring on November 10th. Marshal, have you met Lorenzo and Lillian Stone and their twins, Louis and Lois?"

Garth clicked on his mike and replied, "Yes sir. I had a four day assignment up there a couple of years ago and also got acquainted with Lillian's folks whose last name I can't recall but her father owned a sporting goods store called Nick's Sporting Goods and next door to it the mother had a small coffee shop which featured her doughnuts. Both places were closed on Sunday until the afternoon so none of them would miss worship at the chapel."

Colonel P.J. requested permission of Garth and Gloria to use their given names. This was immediately granted. "Garth, the Senator and I are well aware of your desire to morally and legally do everything you can to preserve her family. And if Lorenzo and his family do decide to live in the Stone house and have their children taught in the village school, you would in no way violate the old treaty by also residing there for they would be eligible to become temporary guardians to Gloria's youngster and you and they could hire her as a live-in housekeeper. However if you try to move in alone as a bachelor, the Browns could not and Gloria would not even be able to legally rent lodging until she is 21.

"So we have a dilemma based on archaic laws and regulations and only God can show us the right moves to take. Dear lady, I have a Calvinist background, and I am convinced without any reservation that there is no situation, no matter how hopeless and helpless it may seem to be, that God, if he so chooses, can make the way clear. Just remember what your Granny said that you must never give in and never give up."

The Tri-motor made several complete tours of the island and as the mother saw the beautiful steep hilled northern half, she couldn't help but silently praise her Heavenly Father or the beauty and splendor of what he had made. And she was also amazed how seeing things from above revealed so much majesty. But she had a very divided mind for it began to look like in spite of the beauty she saw and how the two important men and Garth tried to encourage her, her thoughts kept sinking down to what would surely be the loss of her children. She wanted to hang on to her hope, but her faith was going to an ever lower ebb tide.

Most of the way back to the Crawford Airport there were comments through the earphones from various passengers and the cockpit pair of interesting sights but the Marshal remained very quiet as he pondered just what possibilities he might have to be involved in, to what lengths he might have to go to keep the Brown together. Garth remained silent about his final answer regarding the new assignment available to him.

If his cousin Lorenzo with family came, it might have been possible for Gloria to serve as a housekeeper and not face a parting with her loved ones. If that happened, Garth's residence in the Stone house would not have any bearing on the situation until the magic age of 21 came around. Thus it was feasible that the Marshal could have a permanent residence at Camp Eagle. However if his cousin didn't come there would be no legal possibility of keeping the family trio together or of him living in the Stone house. And also he did not know what would become of the young woman.

The only advantage would be that he would at least not be in some far state.

Although Gloria had brought along her cane in Garth's machine, she had left it there for the healing of her ankle had proceeded even better than the Doctor had expected. Had she been walking and on her legs the biggest share of the time, after a few hours discomfort leading to pain would have been inevitable. But she had spent almost all the time seated since leaving home. Thus when the Tin Goose landed and taxied close to the mess hall, she had almost no noticeable limp. Then the four entered the main building for use of its facilities and some fresh coffee and comments about what had been seen.

Garth was in no way pressured to tell his decision regarding becoming the Commander of Camp Eagle but he quite succinctly announced he would be honored to accept the position and whatever lodging was offered to him. And then he changed the subject and said, "I did enjoy the tasty lunch we had but I crave a more substantial supper and I would like to celebrate what is really quite a promotion by insisting I be allowed to take us all out for supper. A while back I had a very fine meal at Armstrong's Café. And for those who like breaded pork chops, there isn't a better place to go. It's only about a mile from here. I heard the Senator and Colonel talking about spending the night here to continue military budget considerations and I will be glad to drive us all to the Café and bring the two gentlemen back here"

The foursome arrived at the restaurant a bit earlier than the traditional supper hour but they each had better appetites after the light lunch. And despite any gloom which prevailed in the mother when there seemed to be no possible solution to her dilemma, the three-sided encouragement did tend to buoy up her spirit quite a bit. As they had their meals, the two older men shared anecdotes which usually brought laughter to the table.

On their way home the pair from Stillwell had a chance to discuss the impact on the lady of her big adventure off the ground and she rehearsed with him just how she would share it with the children and close friends. She hoped she would have a chance on Wednesday to visit Penny and tell how there were people in important positions in the military and government who were determined that there had to be changes in many oppressive state laws. But she was sure she would bend the healing woman's ears over her "pioneer flight."

Each day of Penny's hospital stay Burly would manage to pop in to visit her at least a couple times and he didn't verbalize it just then that his days seemed empty if he didn't hear her voice or see her unbandaged lower face and its smile which shone on him every time he was there. After she was able to see his face, she would also tell how incomplete her days seemed when his work required him to be absent all day.

The day from morning to suppertime had been blessed by clear skies and mild breezes. But as sunset had approached, the temperature had begun dropping into the freezing zone and the sky quickly filled with angry clouds. An intermittent drizzle began which in some areas was more sleet than rain. This caused occasional small stretches of streets and sidewalks to get slippery. By midnight the prevailing temperature had begun rising back to normal and icy patches began to melt away.

Garth was a driver who had been through enough severely bad driving conditions to drive slower and more alertly when weather flukes came. But he also was quickly aware that the car's heater would soon need attention for the vehicle was becoming quite chilly. And he sensed that his passenger's autumn coat was not keeping her warm.

He slowed down and pulled into the Standard Oil station to check the anti-freeze. Right next door to the station was the place where Burly had taken Penny. Garth said, "Let's have hot chocolate to keep the chill off us and also bring home a bag of their super doughnuts for the kids and us and the O'Connors. Burly, too, okay?"

It sounded good to her. After the necessary checking of the car, he pulled into the lunchroom and parked so her door was right next to the entrance. He came to her door and offered his hand to steady her but she left her cane in the car. They sipped small cups of hot chocolate. She told him it was only a few steps from the entrance to his car so she could get in as he got the pastries.

The lunch room floor was a few steps higher than the drive but it had metal railings on each side. Gloria's shoes had leather soles which had been dampened from the few paces to go in and they were slippery. And there was a bit of slickness at each end of the steps where a bit of ice had accumulated. She had not put her gloves on and her right hand slid on the right railing. Her right foot slid out from under her and she fell feet first under the running board, thumping her hip and shoulder as she went down. Involuntarily she let out a fairly loud moan as she landed.

Garth heard her outcry and turned suddenly and left his sack of doughnuts on the counter and sprinted to the door and went down on his knees beside her to slide her legs out from under the running board. He gently lifted her to a sitting position and asked how bad it was. She said she was just shook up but really okay. She reached her left arm around his neck as he supported her enough to get her standing up and then carefully opened her door and assisted her entry.

The proprietor rushed frantically out to offer any assistance he could and rather incoherently said, "There must have been some ice. I didn't know. I would have thrown salt on the steps. I'll take the blame. Lady, how bad are you hurt? I'll call an ambulance. I can get a doctor here for you. What can I do?"

Garth began to speak but never finished a sentence before Gloria opened her window and said to both men, "I'm really okay except I scratched my palm and I did twist my ankle some. But it can't be serious. Look how I can wriggle my foot. And both of you look like my kids do when they're scared because they did something wrong and they're both ready to bawl. And Sir, there was only a little bit of ice but I stepped right on the middle of it. Will both you guys lighten up? But I do want to thank both of you for being ready to help. A woman doesn't need to be worried when there are two gallant men like you so ready to help her."

She reached out her window to shake the man's hand but first he examined her palm and said, "I have a first aid kit under the counter and I really ought to bandage those scratches. It'll just be a jiffy. And Marshal, come and get your bag of doughnuts and they're on me and your chocolate, too."

The motor had been left running during the above and the car had warmed up considerably. The man insisted she allow him to bandage her palm. The woman would have been very satisfied to just hurry home in spite of her now uncomfortable ankle but she was sure it would soon feel better again. However the Marshal insisted they make a quick stop at the hospital emergency room and there she was quickly x-rayed and rebound with a fresh elastic wrap. The physician told her she had actually set her total recovery back a couple of weeks but all should be well before Thanksgiving.

Clancy was working extra hours at the police department due to illness of a night staff officer but Heidi had gladly volunteered to stay with Dharma and the three kids. And the plane riding duo was home well before bedtime. So Gloria was able to tell as much as was pertinent about their day. She also had a couple of pictures of the Tri-motor craft which were supplied to visitors. Mark particularly was impressed that his sister had not only flown through the air but that she had gotten acquainted with very important people who had promised she would receive all of the photos which would come in the mail.

Of course Uncle Garth had to let the three children wrestle him to the floor the same way they had already done to Uncle Burly. There was a unanimous approval of having a doughnut before going to bed and neither any male nor any female refused to participate in this important ritual. All the children were put into their customary beds but Garth stayed with Mark so they could discuss things important to a little boy. Dharma sat reading until Clancy would get home.

Heidi said to Garth, "Mr. Important United States Marshal, will I need to get a court order to have a private conversation with that renowned aviatrix you took gallivanting all day? I don't have much influence on famous people in high places. But there are times when ladies have things to talk about that almost all men just plain can't grasp." And she turned away from him because she didn't think she'd be able to avoid laughing.

Garth was accustomed to Heidi liking to tease her friends and tried his hardest to wear a very serious face and use a similar voice. "Listen to me, you troublemaker. I'm just about ready to get a warrant and throw you both together into solitary confinement. But if you're together, how could it be solitary? Just tell me where you want to be and perhaps I could look the other way when you escape."

"Thank you, big brother. I wanted to drive her to my dad's restaurant and tell her some things she's been wondering about. And I'll see to it she uses her cane. And I know she's had a long day and does need her rest so we'll both keep an eye on the clock and she can fill me in on her dilemma and I want to share some good things and maybe encourage her. Okay?"

As soon as the two were seated with fresh cups of coffee, Gloria summarized as best she could her helplessness to do anything to avoid losing the children. She also expressed her gratitude for the attitude of the three men who'd done all they could to give her a glimmer of light. She concluded, "If Granny and I knew at the beginning what liars and cheats the two partners were, there never would have been a fake marriage and none of this would be happening to us. But I am determined never to give in or give up. It's not settled until God says it is."

Heidi suggested that Gloria ought to call Pastor Lemunyon from the Nazarene church just on a chance there might be a possibility The Good Shepherd Shelter might be able to somehow be able to help. Unfortunately it was at capacity and also they were restricted by state law from making arrangements for children over eight years old.

Heidi responded, "If only you had known before Maggie was born and there had been someone who loved you and would love Maggie just because she was yours. Oh, I'm dreaming. But I have to tell you how one of my dreams is aimed at being fulfilled."

Gloria interjected, "Herbie?"

"You always were sure it would be him, weren't you?"

"I never expected any other possibility. You said yes?"

"Of course I did. And he gave me an engagement ring but I promised I wouldn't wear it publicly until my folks let everyone know. And here it is." With that she pulled a silver chain up out of her blouse and on it was a gold ring with a small diamond. The stone was quite small. A small income had been pinched for a long time to get the ring. But to the pair of excited women it seemed magnificent.

Gloria asked, "When will it be publicly announced?"

"Sunday, October 24th, at the morning service. Pastor Michaels is going to have an insert made for the bulletin and it is going to tell that on the following Sunday afternoon there will be an open house at Swede's restaurant if any wish to give personal congratulations or should it be called condolences?"

Gloria lightly slapped her friends and said, "Idiot! It's Herbie that needs our sympathy." Then she hugged her and whispered, "I can't tell you how glad I am for you. But is there a date set?"

"After we complete next summer's classes and get our diplomas together. But I sincerely wish you might beat me to a date or some little miracle that lets you keep the kids.

Back at what was still Gloria's apartment; Garth was saying good night to Mark who could hardly keep his eyes open after their little conversation which mostly had to do with airplanes and flying. The lad squinted at his hero and asked if they could sometime the next day talk again because he had some more questions to ask. "I give you my word I'll make my best effort to do just that, partner." The lad zonked out almost immediately.

The following morning Garth gave Gloria a ride to the Nightingale Hospital to visit Penny. Mark had already gone to school and Maggie was delighted to go with Uncle Garth for a little ride. Penny was pleased to announce that the healing of her eyes was ahead of schedule and she could be released for home care to Erica Pulaski on Friday Morning. Then Gloria unfolded her plan to her newest friend who thought it to be good.

"So the Marshal said he would take me apartment hunting today. If I can get you to sign for a place this week, I'll move out a week before the final eviction day and the judge said that anybody that leaves early gets a rebate, even me. So with the rebate and the considerable cash paid to sell out what belonged to me but that we won't let the banks have I'll be able to pay at least a month's rent. Then as soon as you leave Erica's you could move in with the kids and me until we all leave. And you would get the gas stove and fridge and the washing machine because I think the place will only have minimum furnishings."

When Garth went to get Gloria, who was faithfully using her cane, Maggie said excitedly, "Mommy, Uncle Garth took me in a candy store and look what he got me because I was good and drank my whole glass of chocolate milk." And with that she held up an open box of Cracker Jacks and offered a taste to her mother.

The Marshal went about two blocks west from the hospital to Kaufman's Economy Rentals and showed Gloria a first floor partly furnished flat with three small bedrooms, a complete bathroom, a small living room, and somewhat cramped cooking and eating space. The flat was shabby but quite clean. And down the hallway which connected several smaller flats and a laundry room was also the back entrance which opened into a fenced yard where children could play. Gloria gave the landlord a small cash deposit and went away with a lease which needed signing.

That same day a long distance call came from Eagle Island for Garth. It was from his older cousin he called Uncle Rudy asking if the two of them could visit and take the Browns out with for supper. But they insisted that they were planning on staying in a hotel as a special treat they seldom had. So they would actually be coming to Stillwell only three days after the Browns moved.

The Browns insisted Garth be supper guest and Mark reminded the man that he had questions for him. They were not about airplanes. "Uncle Garth, are wishes something like when you tell Jesus there's something you'd really like to get or see?"

"Mark, tell me first what made you think of that?"

"I ate my cake and blew out my candles and my sister Gloria has always said it's just a fun part of birthday parties. And it was really fun but not magic when all the kids and me had rides on ponies."

"Mark, when there are good things we want to happen to us or other people, I am sure Jesus agrees with us. But sometimes he and the Heavenly Father know of other things that are really better for us and they surely won't want to give us things that are bad for us. And many wishes people have might be real bad. Does that help a little so you can understand?"

"Yes sir. But I don't see how one thing I've wished for and prayed for forever can be bad."

"If you've told him about it many times, and you want me to, I will be glad to be a prayer partner with you. That means we'll both be asking him about it but it won't necessarily be at the same times; just when we think of doing it. Does that sound okay? Will you tell me what it is?"

"Yes, Uncle Garth. I never met my real mommy or daddy. But I have seen pictures of them. Sister is almost a mommy to me but not really. It seems like the kids I know have at least one and a lot of times two and I don't have any. Is that too big a wish to tell to Jesus?"

Garth choked up over the heartache he saw in this little boy and tears were ready to flow as he thought of what an awful thing it would be if such a thing as separation happened. He hugged the boy and said, "It would make me proud to have you as a prayer partner. So I'll wish you goodnight now and you hug your sister Gloria real hard before you get in bed." The lad's wish stayed in Garth's mind the way fictional ghosts haunt folks. What could a Marshal do about such a dilemma?

Burly helped Penny get situated at Erica's on Friday, October 22nd. He and Clancy also helped the Browns move on Monday, the 25th. When the Eagle Island Stones arrived on Wednesday afternoon Gloria was only slightly frantic about some of the disorder that remained from getting settled. But to the children, it was all a great adventure, not the least of which was going out to a restaurant where they were allowed considerable choice. Miss Brown acted as hostess and kept Uncle Rudy and Aunt Liz very amused with her account of flying and also showed the photos which had been mailed to Garth.

Then as soon as the children were bedded down, the talking shifted to the great injustice the Child Protective Agency was determined to carry out and how Garth literally had his hands tied preventing any legal action by him. Another injustice would be how a committee manned by loyal employees of the agency assisted by a local judge who had a questionable reputation regarding graft had also ruled that Miss Penelope Harmonia Worthington would be not allowed to testify since she was a disgruntled former employee. This restriction would also be applied to any outside legal interference from lawyers. And Gloria, the obvious offender and lawbreaker, could be present at the hearing but could not be sworn in to testify. Uncle Rudy said that it was nothing but a kangaroo court.

And then he changed the subject. "I want to talk about something else. I love to read history and I want to converse a few minutes about mail-order brides. As the west was being settled there were a lot more men than women. It was a tough life and more women than men died, often leaving behind youngsters. So the survivors who were living lonely lives or had children they couldn't properly care for wrote to what some call lonely heart clubs and often convinced lonely or desperate women out east to come and be a legal wife. Quite a few did and the success rate of the marriages that were entered into was very remarkable. I have mixed emotions about such things but arranged marriages also do have a good success rate.

"And in the Bible we read about father Abraham who sent a trusted servant to travel to the old country and bring back a bride for his son. This was done and the story tells that the son loved his bride. And history is full of arranged marriages which joined royalty from different countries so the two lands could have peace and not war. And this often worked very well."

Garth asked, "So what are you suggesting should be done? If I could help in these matters, I'd be willing to try. But we can't deny that what is done must also be best for all three of the Browns. Only God can give the right answer; I don't know if I would know it if I saw it. I'm not very smart when it comes to love and marriage."

Gloria made friends very easily and she had instantly liked the couple. They had grandchildren and had a farm background and manners that the kids also instantly responded to. She also pondered what the man had been implying. Heidi had also been hinting that one could never outguess what God had in mind. Liz had been doing the most yawning and finally had flat out told her man to put his coat on and head to the hotel for it was getting late.

Before they left for their hotel, Gloria asked if they could possibly do her a big favor. She told them how the only things moved from storage at Erica's to her new lodging had been the washing machine and her cedar chest which had fit on the floor of one of the bedroom closets. "But my dressing table and stool, the foot powered sewing machine, and several boxes of books and such which Granny had are still there. We did move Maggie's bed and a few other things but I don't see that I'll ever need most of the rest and maybe later some of the villagers could get good use of the rest. Could you take them to the Stone house for temporary storage?"

That night Garth was very restless. He had been reviewing his calendar and had made arrangements to rent the room until Wednesday the 10th of November instead of leaving on Saturday October 30th which had been his plan before his new job offer. This would also give him a breather to help Burly get Penny moved in with Gloria and he could arrange temporary lodging in Ottawa Village. And he still didn't know what he could do on November 13th, the custody hearing date.

He knelt down to keep his promise as a prayer partner and while kneeling flipped open his Bible to Isaiah and in his mind came God's question and he remembered how often he had renewed his statement to God, "Here I am. Send me." But the Bible had a marker in it from a recent sermon in which a man of God had accused David and said, "Thou art the man."

CHAPTER EIGHT

On Thursday, October 28th Dr. Isaac Echenstein declared Penny's eyes were up to normal and ordered lightly tinted spectacles to deal with bright lights. She was more excited than she could tell for this would be the first time she could clearly see the face of her hero Burly. Her room in Erica's house was not brightly lit yet. It did have heavy drapes but they were only cracked open a few inches and the reduced daylight was adequate for whatever she needed to do. She had been primping like a girl going to her first prom and although the man was not even a minute late when he arrived, the clock had seemed to be creeping twice as slow as a snail.

She softly said, "Hush for a moment. Just stand tall and don't you dare slouch. Keep your hands out of your trouser pockets and let me memorize your face. I never imagined the man I consider to be the kindest friend I know would also be so handsome."

This little speech so flustered him he couldn't form words to tell her how he couldn't even begin to express his reaction to her grace and charm. But he had no chance to get a sentence out when she said, "Remember that I have a license to teach and when I tell a child to hush, they do it. Not a word out of you right now and I want you to just stand tall and close your eyes. I have something for you which I hope might be acceptable. I want to thank you for how you've done so much to cheer me and made me feel like life is really worth living. I can't thank you enough, my dear friend."

Burly properly played the role of an obedient student but actually stood there like a soldier at attention. She moved up close to his left side and gently took hold of his upper arms and leaned very close so that the light perfume she had used almost enchanted him. But then she turned her face enough so she could place a kiss on his cheek. He was flabbergasted, but secretly delighted.

Up in Ottawa Village the mostly half breed families had for several years been advancing into the modern age. As soon as a power line came across beside the train tracks, the villagers had been subscribing to electrified homes so that now at least three quarters of the homes at least had electric lights. And only a few years later the phone company also provided access so virtually every small business and also Mayor Tootoosee and the depot could call out or be called. But pending the final disposition regarding the coming Eagle Camp, the Stone house did not yet have power or phones although there was a pole adjacent to the house and ready to be hooked up for both services. Thus on Saturday following the visit from the Stones from Eagle Island, a call came to what had been Granny's Lodging for Garth to call Tootoosee as soon as possible.

After the customary greetings the Chief said, "Son, I have bad news and good news but I'd better give the bad first. Your cousin Lorenzo and his family are not going to be able to come. My heart goes out to them but his wife's father had a heart attack and is gone. But he left a will giving his entire estate to his only child, his daughter Lillian but with a proviso that her mother must be provided for or nothing goes to his girl. Well, will or no will, that is exactly what she would have insisted anyhow and Lorenzo agrees. So now he is sole proprietor of Nick's Sporting Goods and his wife very willing to assist her mother with the coffee shop. The children will be starting school next year and I know you join with me in sending our condolences and encouragement. But that also means, since Rudy and Liz are leaving the Stone House for retirement on the ninth of November, we are bound by our ancient treaty to deny you a residence as a bachelor. So there is no way that I know that can stop the stupid politicians from stealing Gloria's children from her. I feel a lot like an Apache and have an urge to go on the war path. God forbid any such stupid moves."

The Chief's bad news made the Marshal's heart feel like ice. "Now how about a bit of good news?" he asked.

"Rudy wants you to know that his son Albert married an orphan gal he met in church in Cleveland. He is a shoe salesman and a cobbler and some other cousin in Livingston, Montana wants a partner. Al and Gracie came by train to Eagle Island but hoped they could ride to Stillwell in that Amish-type coach and have Jesse and Belle pull it there if you could drive it back here since you have to be here for a while part of the time anyway and you have to return that lender Ford to the Sheriff…Wow!... I gotta catch my breath…. Any how we know the government will see to it you get a car, probably from the dealer in Southport, and it would be good if it had the four wheel drive."

Garth asked, "What day did you say they'll be leaving?"

"He said it would be Tuesday, the ninth, of November. Al and Gracie were gonna help them load up the moving van and then enjoy the buggy drive. They hope to see you before they catch their train the next day and they'll be staying at the same hotel. One more thing is that the team will be left at Gene Rogers Livery where we've only heard good things about his treatment of animals."

At the Lutheran Church Sunday, to which Garth drove the Browns, the most remembered words the man recalled later were those spoken to him by Heidi after he reiterated his congratulations that she and Herbert Wilson were going to tie the knot.

Herbie asked, "Are Marshals anything like the Canadian Mounted Police?"

Garth said, "I think all people involved in law enforcement have many common traits."

Heidi opined, "But don't the Mounties always get their man?"

"That's what is said."

"And don't Federal Marshals usually get their man?"

"We certainly hope so."

She asked quietly as she stared intently into his eyes, "Well then, when are you going to find a man for Gloria who will protect her and the children?" She then did an about face and walked rapidly away dragging her puzzled fiancé along with her. Herbie had a problem understanding what was going on.

No matter what the circumstances were, the young Marshal had never wavered from his determination to always maintain his Christian character and also always do what was legal. But now his mind seemed to have entered a whirlpool of indecision about what he could or should do regarding the Browns.

Early Monday morning he received a message via Burly that it was Penny's first day to dwell with the Browns and she insisted Garth come over for supper. She knew chili was a much favored food and she was going to serve a big pot with oyster crackers and a green salad followed by a light Jell-O dessert. He brought along a card table and a few folding chairs and he was very amused by the looks she and Burly exchanged. He admitted to himself that there could not be very many women in the town who were so vivacious.

After the couple went for a little ride and the children were abed, Garth requested a final cup of coffee before he left. It was then he spent a moment asking if Gloria would like to become a third prayer partner. He said, "I'm sure Mark would be glad if three of us would ask Jesus to fulfill his deepest wish. He asked me to pray to see if Jesus would let him have a real Daddy and Mama. His plaintiff request nearly broke my heart. I wish I could see it happen. But what can I do? I'm not one of the Mounties that always get their man."

Tuesday was to be a concluding day for Garth to personally interview every officer who had taken the courses he had offered. There were several un-married officers all of whom were god-fearing men of good character but even the two with lady friends did not declare they were deeply in love and in casual talk all of them felt that a deep love was a prerequisite of a successful marriage. He spoke to the O'Connors about this that evening and they both insisted that strong love was an absolute necessity of a good union. Thus at their persuasion he set up an appointment for the following afternoon with Reverend and Mrs. Michaels to get a better idea of what he should be hoping to locate if there was to be a man for Gloria.

When Garth arrived he was immediately seated in the kitchen and offered fresh baked apple streusel and coffee with them before they told him to tell everything they ought to hear. He was completely at ease with them when he referred back to the funeral day for Granny and then filled them in on the encounter with Miss Penelope Worthington and also her subsequent complete turnaround because of the uncaring treatment that was going to be thrown at Gloria. He also told them that he had been advised to get the viewpoints of the Pastor and his wife regarding to love and marriage. He mentioned his uncle's cryptic remarks which didn't seem appropriate. How in the world was a Marshal to help?

The pastor began by reminding the man that God is love and all true love comes from Him. "Garth, too many people enter marriage with an opinion that it's a matter of what's it going to give to them. People keep saying they fall in love but true love doesn't make you fall; it elevates you. My wife and I would never deny that there is romance, but what a couple receives from a physical union is actually second in God's Word.

"The highest measure is what the loving ones offer, not what they expect to receive. True love always is based on the decision to forever want what is best for the loved one, no matter what it costs. Our example of true love is when the Heavenly Father and his one and only Son agreed together to shed his blood and die in order that we might have forgiveness and eternal life. So those examples your uncle gave were good ones. First came the decision and this might be followed by physical love.

"Using God's standard of decision to insure the betterment of the loved one, do you love Maggie? Would you take action to protect her from danger, no matter the risk to you? Emotion would certainly be aroused, but wouldn't it be based on the decisive mind-set you have?"

"Yes sir. As a police officer in Chicago and in my Marshal training I was always taught to instantly respond."

"And what about for Mark, do you love him? Same answer?" He shook his head. He was quite certain where this was going.

But it was the Pastor's wife who now spoke gently to the man. "It's my turn now. Young man, I have no clue as to what you ought to do about Gloria. And my husband and I both have great confusion as to what this tangled up political law expects. And I know Gloria has been a chaste wife, even if she was tricked into believing she was married. And we are very sure you have not had unwarranted romantic ideas about a Christian lady you believed to be married. But we would also like to know if using the love-decision criteria of ever seeking the highest good for her you would say you loved her. Do you?"

The man looked down and then sipped a bit of his now cold coffee before looking up to meet the two set of eyes. He cleared his throat and said distinctly, "In the sense of already having a desire to see nothing but good come to her I have to say I do love her."

The preacher offered advice. "Garth, before you make any decisions, you ought to confer with an attorney lest what you do won't change the adoption crisis. But make wise haste. That hearing is only ten days off. And our phone and phone book are right here if you'd like to be able to move with speed."

It was not until about seven that evening that Attorney James Stillwell had time to confer with Garth. He had explained that he was certain his father Federal Judge Nehemiah Stillwell would be very happy to sign necessary papers regarding the adoption and full parental guardianship over Mark and change of last name for Margaret. But neither of these legal papers would be viable until after a legal wedding certificate was in effect. So it really all depended on whether there would be a wedding. There were obstacles to be overcome. Wedding licenses had to be issued at least forty eight hours before they were valid and there had not yet been a mutual consent to marriage and the license bureau was not open on Saturdays.

Garth had a tough time trying to reason out just what he should do. It came back to him how often over the years he had spoken to God to declare his availability and willingness to follow the Lord's leadership no matter what it required him to do. But there had never even been a hint that God was going to powerfully point him toward possible matrimony. Or had there been? The man of God who said, "Thou art the man," was pointing at a terrible sin in David's life which demanded that King David take specific actions. Could a reluctance to obey God's leading be related? David had disobeyed God's commandment. Could seeking to avoid a union with a woman be the same thing? Are sins of every nature equal?

He discovered he could hardly even pray to fulfill his promise to remind Jesus about Mark's wish to have a daddy. Before he was able to get to sleep that night he had paused to tell the Lord that subject to the answer of the woman, he would do everything that was humanly possible to follow God's leading. As soon as his unconditional surrender to the Shepherd of his soul, he was absolutely at peace and worry was an enemy the Master had expelled so that he had the best rest he could remember.

Mark and Maggie were eating bowls of cereal as the Marshal came ringing the doorbell. He rather exuberantly greeted them. As soon as the children finished eating, Mark headed out to school. Garth then accepted a bowl of corn flakes and the two ladies crunched away with him smiling at his little jokes and glad to see him but puzzled by his unusually high spirits.

Penny asked him, "Did you happen to win some lottery or sweepstakes?"

"Nothing that unimportant. But I have some very important things to discuss with Gloria and I was hoping you could stay with Maggie while we vacate the premises. It really is important and it should be decided as soon as possible."

He ended up driving the woman to what had been Granny's Lodging and took her into the kitchen and shut the doors for private conversation. He sat opposite her at the table and without any preamble said, "I think there is a good way to see to it that the children could be yours until they grow up and get married. I talked with your pastor and his wife and also with Attorney Stillwell. I was given a better understanding of what love is really about and also some very doable legal procedures which will benefit both you and me."

"Let me tell you what the Michaels couple shared with me." She listened and asked him to repeat parts and then replied, "I think I have to agree. Love is much more than taking. It really is about giving and putting others first. I'm sure it's what Jesus said and did. It has to be more about giving than taking."

Garth then summarized the dialogue regarding him, Maggie, Mark, and finally the declaration he'd made that he also loved her. She became very silent. He wondered if what he had told her thus far was shaping her willingness to consider more or felt like it was part of a pipe-dream. He told her about the certainty that there could be binding legal reasons to forever have family security.

He explained that he was certain the Heavenly Father had been planning it all the time. "Think of all the things involved. I was offered a more permanent job which would pretty much keep me in one place. And there are all the little details such as residence and a vehicle etc. But the biggest hurdle for this moment is whether you could possibly have enough of the opening stage of love for me such as I already confessed about you. I know you had immense love for the man who deceived you. But I have to confess that probably neither of us has what most people have in the beginning. I mean romantic love; physical yearning. I think we both trust and respect each other and I know that it goes against all I am to ever want to see you harmed. What do you think of me?"

She got up from the table and turned away from him and stared out the window. Without facing him she was very silent and gripped the edge of the sink as if she was almost too weak to remain standing. After a long pause during which he held his breath, she finally spoke distinctly but very quietly. "Garth, if I made a list of everyone I trust and respect and also consider that I have love for them, your name would be high on the list. I would never want to lose you as my friend. But what do you expect me to do?"

"I want you to answer me a question. And it scares me to think you might say yes. But it also scares me that you might say no. First please sit facing me. I have to see your face."

She had a blur of uncertainty of what the Marshal might ask. He hesitated before asking a simple question, "Gloria, this is probably the poorest proposal any good woman would want to get, but will you marry me?" It shouldn't have taken her by such surprise, but she had not even considered such a wild possibility. And she also was scared of saying yes or saying no. The only reply she had breath to give was that it was so sudden.

And then Garth said, "I know it is. But if we aren't wedded and have the other legal documents before the hearing on the Saturday of the 13th, it might take thousands of dollars of legal fees and months or even years to get the kids back. Is it possible you can give me an answer today? And please speak to the Lord first and then get the word to me this afternoon so I can begin making the legal arrangements if you answer yes."

She said softly, "After Granny died, Heidi was my dearest friend in this world. And I would feel better about it if she knew about this and would pray with me. You know she already is engaged and Herbie even has a wedding ring for her so she has inside wisdom about these matters."

Garth said, "I'm glad you mentioned that ring. The last couple of years before my mother died she had such bad arthritis in her knuckles she had to quit wearing her wedding ring and my dad gave it to me to keep and I forgot to ask you if you would object to wearing it if you say yes. And also I trust Heidi's good sense and her faith and the power of her praying. So do confer with her."

She replied, "You reminded me that when my father died from burns on the ship in Lake Michigan, Granny received his wedding band and it's in my treasure box. My mother's ring was buried with her. But if God leads me to say yes, I would be honored to wear your mother's ring and I hope you will accept my dad's."

He nodded his head in the affirmative and as he did she held up her hand and said, "To show you I promise you a definite answer let us shake hands on it." He shook with her and gave her a ride back to her apartment. To both their surprises, the somewhat beat-up Chrysler which had been abandoned in the drive next to the Agency office was parked in front.

Penny was almost too excited to tell them two good pieces of news. "Just a few days ago Burly had strong words with Mr. Loocerson who was more than happy to sign the title over to avoid repair costs. Burly said the major problem was a voltage control which needed replacing and a few new fuses. He gave the battery a charge and put tape over the leaky window and it's raring to go. Maggie and I rode with him over to the gas station to get it and here it is. The other news is that the Sheriff and Mayor went to speak to the Principle about substitute teaching and I've been promised at least two days' work a week."

Penny was delighted to put on her temporary sunglasses and to give Gloria a ride to Swede's to confer with Heidi and later to pick up Mark at school and give both children a ride while the two younger ladies had a serious time together. She very much enjoyed that she was now Auntie Penny to the kids. It made her feel even closer to Uncle Burly than before.

Just before supper time at Swede's Nels called Garth to ask him to come over and get Gloria who was going to wait for him in the small private dining room. Judging by the time to get there, one could suspect the Marshal did not concern himself with speed laws.

Gloria grasped his gun hand and hastened him in. Without hesitation she began, "When you asked me my first thought was you had to be kidding. But the way you looked into my eyes made me know you were dead serious. And a powerful conviction came over me that you weren't some love stricken beau but you were actually a spokesman for God. I was scared because I already knew what the reaction of my soul would have to be but I just didn't know if I could really be a good wife to you. Yes! I'll say it again. Yes!"

They agreed the very next order of business was to see Attorney James Stillwell that very day so there could be no delays in all the legal paperwork. He congratulated them and also told them that his father, the Federal judge, was already at work with injunctions and orders to cancel the hearing regarding taking the children and also that he would be in communication with J. Edgar Hoover regarding investigating graft and unconstitutionality of some of the state law. They left the lawyer's office amazed at some of the unknown extent of what was undoubtedly the hand of God moving behind the scenes. They also decided not to tell Mark or Maggie until they visited with Reverend Michaels regarding their use of the sanctuary for their nuptials.

The betrothed couple met with the Pastor and his wife as early as possible after breakfast. Quickly they told of their decision and begged use of the church for their wedding. Mrs. Michaels said, "We were so sure about this we already made calls so everything would be ready for your wedding service at nine o'clock Thursday. And I will be serving the four of you breakfast at seven. Herman has also prepared the text of the announcement. Let him read it to you."

"Actually my Bertha did the preparing. I'll just give you the gist of it. This is going to be a very low budget wedding. A half hour is allowed for the service but none of our budgets permit a luncheon reception. Only those actually involved will be taken aside for signing documents and then given punch and a small piece of wedding cake after which my wife and Gloria's choice of helper will aid in packing away the wedding gown and getting her into her traveling duds. Those who attend the service will have to be patient until the bride and groom are ready for the congratulation line. Hopefully it will be not later than ten o'clock. Herbert Wilson is quite an amateur photographer and we were sure that he would be allowed to take pictures for a wedding album with the camera that was left behind for Gloria. One last thing I must mention is that Penny Worthington, whose seldom mentioned middle name is Harmonia, will be providing background music of hymns which anyone may join in as they are waiting in the sanctuary. Well, what do you both think?"

Garth said, "I'm scared." Gloria echoed his exact words.

The preacher chuckled and said, "I am too. We only have a few weddings each year and my tongue gets all tangled up. But nobody dares laugh at such an imposing fellow as me." At this Bertha lightly jabbed him in the rib with an elbow and everyone relaxed.

Bertha asked if they had already picked people for the wedding party. Gloria wanted Nels to give her away, Heidi as Maid of Honor, and Dharma as Bride's Maid. She wasn't sure if there would be a need for a flower girl and the Pastor told her that was a must and he agreed Maggie would be great. Garth then requested Burly as his Best Man and Clancy also. And he had no hesitation in requesting Mark as ring bearer.

It was well before noon when they left the parsonage and the man said he had some shopping to do and he had already spoken to Erica about an appointment for the woman who had agreed to be his wife. "Ma'am, she told me she insisted you have the full treatment, shampoo, haircut, and a permanent as a wedding gift to you. She said you have a beautiful head of hair and after while it was gonna be my task to brush it for you and that idea really scares me. But if you'll be patient with me I'd certainly try. It couldn't be much worse than curry-combing a horse, could it?"

She couldn't avoid laughing but also made a loose fist and swung at his shoulder and whispered one of Granny's oft repeated jokes. "Men! Phooey! You cain't live with 'em and you cain't live without 'em."

He completed his shopping and still had time for a well-needed haircut until she was done. She very much approved of the gifts for the children to receive before the trip to the Stone house. But he had also gotten her a silver brooch made of two interlocking hearts to wear on the journey and then whenever. And they both agreed the children were not to be told of the wedding plans until after the License was safely purchased and in the preacher's hands. But their thinking was flawed for Mark heard about it at church.

Garth quickly explained that Jesus wanted the boy to have his wish. "Mark, after the wedding you will have to call me Daddy because I will be him and Maggie will be my little girl and call me Daddy. And your sister will really be mother of both of you. Tell Jesus thank you for granting your wish. Ain't it great how good he is to all of us?"

People often remark that small towns seldom have to publicize news for it so quickly spreads through the grape vine. And everywhere the children and the couple went there were congratulations. The left over time after Sunday worship was full of what was considered good news. It became difficult on the days before the wedding to scurry around fast enough to deal with last minute items such as dry cleaning the wedding gown and getting flowers. It was also very hard to squeeze in time to visit with Al and Gracie Stone and tend to Jesse and Belle.

In days to come Garth did confide to Gloria that he had no memory of the bountiful breakfast Bertha Michaels had prepared for them. He sat across the table from his intended and discovered that it was almost impossible to take his eyes of her. There is folklore that declares that all brides are beautiful in the eyes of their mate-to-be. And Garth was almost amazed that he had never before really noticed the radiance her face seemed to exude.

When Lars gallantly escorted her down the aisle, the very old-fashioned long-skirted gown and her veil did nothing to take away from her dignity and grace. The old carefully preserved high shoes were enough to keep her ankle from causing her a noticeable limp. To the man's eyes she seemed like royalty. When he finally removed her veil, he wondered how she could possibly have seen anything good in him. He did remember them placing rings on each other's ring fingers. He only vaguely recalled later how soon it seemed that the Reverend had pronounced them to be husband and wife and introduced them to the large number in the sanctuary.

The church parsonage was adjacent to the rear entrance of the church. The narrow driveway led to the garage for the pastor's car. It had been the pastor's dining room where the breakfast had been served and also the home where the new Stone family would come to change into their travelling clothes. Gene Rogers had backed in the buggy drawn by Belle and Jesse who would later be introduced to the children and bride.

After the papers were all in order and the photos taken and the wedding party had cake and punch and the line had gone by, it was time to change clothes for the trip to the Island. Gloria wore a warm woolen dress but also had feminine long underwear, a sweater, high woolen stockings, and a warm kerchief, besides conventional shoes and rubber over shoes. Her winter coat should keep her warm enough but the weather report had been that along the vicinity of the Eagle River it might approach zero late at night and would almost certainly have a few inches of snow before morning.

The children were perhaps not very willingly made to wear long underwear under customary play clothes which included sweaters and overcoats. And the Marshal used red flannel under his working uniform in which he had first dined with Gloria. His badge was prominent on his overcoat and those in the know could tell his holster was concealed on his hip.

Just before departure, he gave packages to his three passengers. He gave to Maggie a used doll in good condition. "Sweetheart, the lady at the store said her name was Sleepyhead Suzie but you can give her a new name. When you hold her up, she looks around but when you lay her down her eyes close. And she is in her pajamas and here's her blanket to keep her warm. But also I got you some nice warm mittens and they're red so you can find them in the snow if you drop them. I'm your new Daddy and I love you so much."

Her response was to hand Suzie to her mother so she could grab him with a mighty child's hug and said, "I love you, too, Daddy. Thank you, thank you, and thank you." And then she gave him a sloppy big kiss on his cheek before taking her new doll back from her mother.

Garth turned to the boy and handed an odd shaped package to him. "Mark, you must not call me uncle ever again. I am now really and truly your Daddy. And I love you very much and have a package for you." The lad was almost crying as he said with tremulous words, "I love you, too, Daddy. And thank you so much no matter what's in this package."

Inside was a shiny pair of lined leather gloves such as buggy drivers wore to get a good grip on reins when racing. But there was also a brand new ell shaped flashlight with a belt clip such as boy scouts sometimes have. The lad was full of wonder that Jesus had filled his wish and then added extra he had never dreamed possible.

Next Garth handed a package to his wife. She was wearing the silver twin heart brooch and had not thought there would be any other gift. But within was a long scarf which could double as a shawl and feminine leather gloves. "I didn't expect more, Mr. Stone. Thank you so much." "Well I couldn't remember where the curry combs were, Mrs. Stone…. Okay everyone. Say bye-bye and thank you to the Michaels. And we're on our way and it's only eleven o'clock. Kids get in back. Mrs. Stone will ride up front for a while."

As they started out she murmured to him, "I wasn't thinking straight. I should have got you a gift." "Mrs. Stone, you couldn't have given me more. Sitting in the back is my proof. I was a single man and you gave me a family. And would you mind tooting the ah-ooga horn? It sticks outside and all you have to do is squeeze the rubber ball inside to warn others about a woman driver and then take the reins for a while. I've already heard from Mr. Rogers that you know how to drive a buggy."

At about eleven thirty he thanked her and she slid the reins back to him through the slot at the bottom of the windshield. Both children had curled up together and were napping in back until nearly one o'clock when the man stopped in the parking area of Schmidt's Dining Room. Garth helped Gloria down and irregardless of her cane, put his arm around her waist to steady her but sent the children in first.

The host and owner was Clifford Schmidt who led them to a pleasant table near the rest rooms. As they followed the husky man who assisted the woman and children to be seated, a cheery rather stout woman waved to them in welcome and they saw her name tag which identified her as Maude Schmidt, obviously the wife. She quickly sent her daughter Rebecca over with menus. Gloria said, "I think my children and my husband are as hungry as I am. What do you recommend?"

The waitress convinced them a family style meal of beef stew with dumplings and their beverages was the best for the money with as many repeat servings as were wanted and it would include some simple desserts. Any two dinners ordered separately would have cost more without dessert or children's portions. The cook who had greeted them was almost an equal to what Granny had been. And the new family noticed that the dining room had people coming and going and seldom had less than one third of the seats occupied. Then when the very friendly host came over with the check and a bag of cookies for dessert, he commented to the couple how marvelously the children had behaved and asked how long they had been married.

Garth explained, "Her man was suddenly taken and we were just married at about nine thirty this morning. Give her full credit for an amazing job of mothering. But I'm their Daddy now. And please compliment the cook and our waitress."

Before the Stone family had time to use the rest rooms, two very noisy cars with three intoxicated rowdy young men in each came squealing to a stop. The foul-mouthed gang leader shoved Clifford to the side and demanded to go to the bar. But this restaurant had no bar and would do no more than serving beer or wine with a meal.

Garth spoke loudly to the legitimate patrons. "Please remain in your seats and refrain from unnecessary talking. I am a Federal Marshal and in a moment or two this situation will be entirely different. Now I'm ordering you six all to sit down at that table and listen to me." The one who thought he was really tough and the boss of the little gang refused to sit; the other five were sober enough to feel fear. The so-called leader remained standing and slowly pulled a folding knife from his pocket. Garth said, "Haven't you ever heard that only a fool will bring a knife to a gun fight?" And with a deft move the lawman flipped his coat open and unsnapped the holster holding his 9 MM. "Mr. Schmidt, call the State Police and see how quickly they can be here. I will personally press charges against this one man if he doesn't surrender his weapon. And since all of you are probably drunk enough to be violating the drunk driving limits, all the vehicles will be impounded. And don't any of you dare to use obscene language in a public place again when women or children are present."

The State Police Post was only a few hundred yards down the road and six arrests were quickly made and wreckers called. Five would be released in the morning. The other faced a charge of assault against the owner and a second charge relating to drawing a concealed weapon to threaten a Federal Officer.

When the Stone family was preparing to leave, Rebecca came rushing out with a bag with a half dozen apples and also a little bag of jelly beans. She said, "Two of the apples are for the horses; I love horses. The candy and other apples are for you guys however you want to split them up. And there's no way we can thank you enough for keeping everybody safe."

The brand new father now gave two apples to each of the children and gave them formal introductions to Belle and Jesse so each child could pet each horse and talk to them and give each of them a treat. They were then placed up front side by side so Garth could talk to them. Both of them had seem pictures of knights in armor on horses and the man explained to them about how the Magna Charta had come about.

"And then since all the kings had castles, it was decided that fathers could call their homes castles and bad people couldn't just come in and rob and hurt the family. And since kings had wives that were queens, our home will be our castle and your mother is the queen, and I am the king, and Maggie is our princess and Mark is our prince and that is just like a knight. And he will always help me to protect the rest of us."

Every so often they found little pullover places to park and there were usually picnic tables and outhouses which could be used. As it began to get dark and colder Garth lit two lanterns on the top front corners of the roof. These had red glass in back but only shone white light about forty feet ahead. On the back of the closed buggy was one small lamp with all red glass he also lit. Outside behind the rear seat was a sturdy rack where the cedar chest and suitcases were securely strapped in and then covered by heavy canvas which was tied in place. The coach had front and back hinged doors on the curb side and auto glass flat sliding windows on both sides. There was also a bracket on the rear floor close to the middle of the front seat which securely held a small lantern which was surrounded by mesh like a small birdcage. The little light only dimly lit the back seat but its meager heat output greatly alleviated chills in cold weather. There were also several large quilts to give passengers or drivers protection in cold times which had been predicted for later that evening.

At around seven thirty at a quick stop he moved Maggie in back and made sure they were well bundled up against the increasing chill. He also gave quick instructions to Mark and allowed him almost a half hour of driving time wearing the new gloves. As Mark began to be chilled his new father praised him immensely for what had been done and wrapped him extra warm and told him to nap if he could and that he needn't worry about the horses getting too cold. He said, "When wild these horses have extra heavy fur that keeps them warm. But any horse that is pulling a load stays much warmer than if they're just standing."

It was after ten when they crossed the covered bridge and soon saw the glimmer of a big lantern which had been hung up between the big barn doors. As soon as the team saw the distant light it was almost impossible for the man to prevent them from picking up the pace to get in, not away from the cold but to their stall and the hay and oats that were waiting. Garth had made sure everyone was awake after they left the covered bridge.

The barn had two doors wide enough to easily accommodate wider farm implements or wagons heavily loaded with bales. And the doors were very recent sturdy overhead doors. The man hopped out of the coach and raised the southernmost door to lead the team in and then hung the lantern on a hook between the doors before pulling the door shut. On the center of the residence was a low porch with both steps and a ramp. Large double doors with glass panes permitted light from the lantern into the hall. The three lamps on the roof of the coach added enough illumination so that the spacious barn did not seem so spooky to Maggie.

He led the team around in a half circle to the other barn door and then backed them up until the doors of the coach were quite close to the porch steps. Garth helped the boy out of the coach and said to his son, "I need your help, partner. You and I have to unbuckle the horses' harness and dry them a bit. Then I need a handyman with a flashlight to shine in their double stall so I can light a little lamp in there. Horses don't need much light, but we do to tend to them after dark if it's needed. Shine your light toward the house so I can light the lamp. See that stone wall. There are chimneys in it from the basement stove and the big Franklin stove. And see that hay rack and those smaller kettles that have oats in the? And see the watering trough fastened to the wall and the little pitcher pump next to the wall? Well in the coldest of winters, even if the barn needs to be open, that chimney wall always stays warm and none of that water ever freezes."

The man showed Mark how to hold Belle's halter to lead her into her side of the stall the same way he led in Jesse. He then called to Gloria, "Mrs. Stone, this son of ours is a remarkable helper. But we have to go in and get lights going and stoke some stoves before we'll be able to allow our Queen and Princess to enter. His flashlight is a great help in getting around doing things."

It was nearly eleven before the inside chores were dealt with. The wind was by then howling and the temperature plummeting. The west side of the house was quite cold for all the old plaster lath had been stripped and new insulating partly done. All the double hung windows that side had to be taken down and although the storm windows were up many of them were quite drafty. But narrow tongue and groove paneling had arrived and was in the process of being stained prior to application. Where it had been considered necessary to do so; sheets had been tacked up to block strong drafts from the lower halves of windows.

The father was accompanied by Mark and instructed Maggie to take his hand and wait right inside the door. "And maybe you should hold Suzie up straight so she can see her new home. Hold Mark's hand, sweetheart." He then asked Gloria to slide across the seat and inquired of her ankle to which she told him it hardly ever ached any more. "I would like it if you would do me a favor for a couple of minutes. Close your eyes tight and don't peek. It's an old custom that a new husband ought to carry his bride across the threshold. So duck your head under this door frame and hang on tight in case I'm clumsy. And promise me you won't open your eyes until I tell you."

She thought that relating to clumsiness, she had once seen a circus acrobat who wasn't nearly ever as steady or sure of his motions as this man she had just wed. And as she was carried up to the door, she heard the kids giggling. They opened the door for her and before she could do anything Garth was setting her down in a heavily cushioned wheel chair and she gasped as the children said surprise. It was not something she needed but at that moment she knew it was a way of showing love to her and thanked all three although she also remembered that Aunt Liz had mentioned that there was one elderly cripple who used it. And just then the Grandfather Clock halfway down the hall chimed out eleven.

Maggie was glad to crawl up on her mama's a lap but let Suzie lay down to sleep. Garth gave the ladies a lightning tour. His office was first on the right. Mark's bedroom was next and Maggie's next to his. Both rooms had small lamps on their dressers but also candles lit until bedtime. The next room was a complete bathroom which also had a small bottled gas water heater. Beyond this was the laundry room which had a coal stove hooked to the same water tank in the attic that the gas stove helped to warm. Next was the pantry. The spacious kitchen had a table big enough for six and a wood burning cook stove but also a bottled gas range and gas refrigerator.

Beyond the kitchen was the spacious screen porch. Windows on the north enabled them through the often swirling snow to see a few lights in the village. Across the hall sliding doors opened to a grand dining room with sitting room. There were several other rooms before arriving at the master bedroom. Then there was the room in which was the Franklin stove and at the west end a couple of cases full of books and a table with chairs. But most prominent was an extra-long sofa facing the stove and a large long mirror on the mantel on which were lighted two lamps.

Gloria said to the children, "This is as big as a mansion. I love it, don't you? And Mr. Stone, I know you said it was God who made the plan, but he made you do most of the work. How can we ever thank both of you enough? And I'm ashamed that I never gave you a gift and you had gifts for all of us."

"What I gave was not really much. I'll never be able to thank you enough, dear lady for all I'm receiving."

Vagrant thoughts went through her mind about how that other man always expected her to be submissive to his every desire no matter how she felt although he had never been brutal until that last evening. Could this very gentle person be expecting her to submit to what so many called a husband's rights?

"Mrs. Stone, in just a few hours today you gave me a gift I can't begin to put a price on. You turned me from a lonesome bachelor into a very happy father. And you pledged with me that we would both ever do the best we could for each other and our children. Now would the three of you sit here in front of the warm stove and maybe shed extra coats and hat and such as I get the lunch Aunt Liz left in the fridge?"

He came back with a cart such as Gloria has used at Swede's to serve them. On it were boxes of saltine crackers, trays of small pieces of cheese and lunch meat stuck on tooth picks, jars of peanut butter and jelly, and devilled eggs. There was also a small covered kettle from the fridge full of cocoa which had been sitting on the wood stove but now was placed atop the parlor stove to finish warming before drinking. And there was a cookie jar full of chocolate chip cookies. And with sips of cocoa Gloria obeyed her doctor's instruction to take pain pills upon arising, at midday, and before bed.

The thoughtful bedtime snack had one kicker to it. As soon as the children ate, bedtime was announced. Pushed by Mark, Gloria rode Maggie with her into the bathroom which was the warmest place to change into pajamas to complete the child's ritual before heading to her room. Both parents were there for tucking in and prayer. Garth was deeply moved as the almost sleeping gal hugged them both but also whispered to him that she loved him and gave him a little kiss.

Mark was well able to use the warm bathroom alone but also wanted two parents to be there for his prayers and tucking in and told both of them he loved them. The long day had pretty well drained him and he was almost out like a light. Then Garth blew out the children's candles and lowered their lamp lights but left the doors open to receive warmth from the stove.

The woman was next to change into her night clothes in the bathroom and left on the long underwear beneath her flannel robe. But she also put on her old faithful quilted robe before returning to the sofa. He asked if they could talk about a few things that were better spoken privately. He told her he knew they were both extremely tired but in his mind these were important matters.

She hardly knew him well and she was apprehensive about whether she would be able to adequately meet his needs. But she also knew her Shepherd never made mistakes.

CHAPTER NINE

By the time Gloria dressed for bed and used the bathroom facilities, Garth had already put away leftovers and also donned his pajamas and robe in the quite cold master bedroom but hadn't shed his red flannels. He shuffled over to the bathroom door in his floppy slippers and wheeled her back to the comfortable sofa where by now it was pleasantly warm. He excused himself from her presence for a few minutes in the bathroom and then came back and inquired about how her ankle felt and whether she would object to him tending to a lighter rewind of the elastic band but first a light massage.

It was necessary for him to slip a foot stool under her heel and then ever so softly lifted the robe and gown nearly to her knee and also bunched up her long under wear after sliding off her right fuzzy slipper and lowering her stocking. In no way was she embarrassed that the lower part of her injured leg was briefly exposed by removal of the elastic band. His careful massage of the injured area was firm enough to aid her circulation but caused no pain. As soon as the bandage and lower leg covering were restored, but a bit looser, she thanked him.

He said, "Mrs. Stone, you're a good patient. But I do have some things I must talk to you about before we both get too sleepy. Sleep is one thing I want to mention. There are enough quilts and such that I could use the single bed in the room beyond the big bedroom if you could get better rest that way."

"I have two questions for you, Mr. Stone. The first is why we should keep saying Mr. and Mrs. to each other? We've been using first names most of the time for several weeks already. Should we talk like strangers do?"

"You're right, Gloria. I agree. I guess I'm just nervous. What's the other question?"

"Is there something wrong with me Garth, which makes you nervous? I think it makes more sense when it's so cold in our bedroom to keep each other from getting too chilly. Maybe I'm nervous too. But I trust you and know you'd never do anything to harm me."

He paused briefly to help her sit up and drew her close beside him and both of them basked in the stove's warmth. "Gloria, would it seem strange to you if I told you things my father told me about love and marriage? It was never about the very private man and wife matters but more about many caring little daily living things." She nodded assent.

"He often told me that all brides are beautiful in the eyes of the men who love them. But I never had any glimmer of understanding about this until we sat across the breakfast table this morning. I had seen you many times before then but now it was almost impossible for me to take my eyes off you. And then when Swede escorted you down the aisle I almost thought you were an angel. Ever since our first meeting, I had always thought you had a glow to you. But

215

now I think you are the most beautiful woman I've ever known."

She was almost speechless and couldn't form a thing to reply. She really wanted to use similar wife's words to a husband for her thoughts were akin to his. But he held his finger to his lips to signal her not to speak because he still had much to say to her.

"My daddy told me often about his one-two-three plan. I really flunked out at church today with it because I'm too naïve about demonstrating the plan. I have to admit my experience with females extends to young cousins and old aunts. I've several times seen you hug Frank, or Dharma hug Clancy and hugging is number one but I'm a klutz with this. Before the pastor said to kiss the bride, I guess I loosely slipped an arm around you but I didn't squeeze you. And a very important part of plan one is the kiss that accompanies the hug. I know our lips lightly touched but I can't even remember what it felt like."

She admitted that to her also the whole service was a big blur. He continued by asking her if she would right then and there teach him to hug her and kiss her. "You've got experience; I really don't. I feel like a helpless dolt. Will you help me?"

She was more touched by his plea of helplessness than by his former declaration that he thought she was beautiful. "You're a big strong man so help me stand up with you and pull me close to you as I do the same thing with you. That's good. Married folks need to draw close to each other. Now close your eyes and turn your head a bit so our noses miss each other. Now we'll push our lips…."

They each soon stopped and opened their eyes and both noticed almost surprise in their partner's eyes. He murmured, "You're a good teacher. Let's try that again. They say practice makes perfect." After a couple of more tries she asked what the other parts of his father's plan were.

"Gloria, he said if you want people to know the truth, it's important to keep telling it to them and in the process of telling it you personally absorb it better. And loving is the most important part of life. Well, my mom's middle name was Belinda but Dad called her Bee. His name was Garrison and she called him Gary. So every day he would say 'I love you, Bee' and she would say to him 'and I love you Gary'. Would you say to me 'I love you, Garth?' I'm planning to say to you 'I love you, Gloria' very often. Does it sound like a good idea?"

She nodded and reminded him how often both of them were accustomed to tell both children they loved them and how often the children responded. "So saying you love someone is the second part of the plan? What's the third?"

"Well, it's sort of a code. Hold my hand and close your eyes." He gave her hand three successive very soft squeezes. "Did you feel that? Those three tiny squeezes which others wouldn't even know happened are a code which says I love you. And they don't have to be on the hand. They might be on an arm or shoulder or back. You'll not have trouble with the plan will you?"

The clock chimed twelve and he said, "We better get ourselves bundled under the covers. But I plan to add wood to the stoves at about three and it should be quite warm in the house by morning. Then I think I'll maybe sleep in until six thirty before I refill the stoves or before I check on the horses."

He circled her waist for extra steadiness to enter their room but also was adamant about her using the cane. The room had adequate light from the small oil lamp which he set for a low flame after blowing out the candle. Gloria stared at the big brass bed and said, "I've never seen one quite as big."

He pulled the covers back on the left side nearest the open door and explained, "My uncle and aunt as you noticed were quite large people and one furniture factory sold them this brass bed which is called King-sized. It would be just right when a new queen and king begin to use it. And you did say you usually slept on your left side which is really best so your right ankle isn't bothered. Now back up toward the center and I'll tuck you in and then I'll sleep facing your back so we'll keep each other warm. And tomorrow night at bed time when it's warmer in the house we can kneel for prayer but I don't think God has any trouble hearing every word even when we're not praying out loud. Good night and I love you, Gloria." Even though she was muffled by the covers, he could hear her whispered reply.

And part of him was incredulous that she seemed to accept him just as he was. After removing robe and slippers he was almost unable to slide under the covers and be in physical contact with her much like nesting two spoons together. Aside from his parents allowing him to slip into bed with them when it was quite cold or if he was scared; he had no memory of ever being in bed with a mature woman. She was already drifting into blessed slumber when he finally had courage to slide his left arm under her pillow and slip his right arm around her waist to prevent her rolling and landing on the floor.

A person who hears clock chimes every hour or half hour often has no trouble awaking at specific times. Thus when he came back after renewing the fires, it was no great surprise that in her sleep his wife had wiggled farther back toward the warm center he had left. Even with the dim lamp on the dresser he could see her face and had to stare at her child-like innocence which had no trace of fear or worry.

In the morning as he pulled coveralls over his pajamas and added sox and boots he noticed that her wheelchair was missing and he heard little noises in the kitchen. He decided that he would tend to the horses before adding wood to the stoves but he also noticed the level of light where she was had been boosted and he faintly heard some quiet humming. He had not had any inkling as to how long she had been up, but there was definitely the enticing odor of coffee cake.

She must have heard him open the Franklin stove and toss in some wood for she backed out of the kitchen in the wheelchair to glance down the hall toward him and then wheeled back in to the counter to finish beating pancake batter. But she was listening intently for the clopping of his work shoes as he came to the kitchen to add wood to the cook stove. Before he could do anything, she rose up and leaned against the table and held out her arms for him. She gave him a quick hug and a kiss and said, "Good morning. And I love you, Garth."

He responded to her actions and words but was puzzled. "Did you have enough rest? How long were you up baking and such?"

"Just a couple of hours. But I think I spent almost half our time on the road grabbing naps so I'm well rested. And I would have been ashamed if you and the children didn't have an extra good breakfast on our first day in our castle. After all you've been doing for us; I don't see how we can ever do enough for you."

By eight thirty all were garbed in every day clothes and necessary bed making and kitchen chores complete. The father had told them Chief Tootoosee was accustomed to knocking on the back door and bringing over eggs, milk, and butter each weekend. Uncle Rudy and many of the village citizens had engaged in barter relating to garden things and also the Stone barn had in it a small but powerful gas motor powered grinder for producing flour or feed. The now retired and absent couple never had any cash differences to consider. The villagers knew Garth also had been able to grind and rumor had it that his bride had gardening skills and canning skills.

At nine Gloria, by now noticing almost no aches in her ankle, did not use the chair but kept using the cane. She and the children hastened to welcome Chief Aaron and his wife Jarinda to have fresh coffee, as did Garth also. The woman was slimmer than her husband but skin tones and shiny black hair gave them similar racial appearances. Jarinda spoke up first. "We are both Indians. But his ancestors were from Michigan and mine from Calcutta. I haven't yet found out if my name has a special translation but the story is that when I was born my mother picked my name because she liked how it sounded. Now don't believe his version of our courtship because as soon as we got acquainted, I made a plan to get him and I won and we have two teen age sons now and two grade school daughters I just know are going to be a handful for us. It's your turn, Aaron."

Without a preamble Aaron first mentioned that all roof work was done. Then he told of a work team of about ten teen-agers and skilled adults. "They're gonna come over at ten today and leave at about five. The rest of the days they'll start at eight, go home for lunch for maybe a half hour and then stay till about six. They should have all the insulating done before they leave Saturday. And then it is fully expected all the tongue and groove wood will be up and the windows properly caulked and sealed before Thanksgiving."

Garth asked, "Do you wish us to feed them at Lunch time?"

Before the chief could answer both kids came flying down the hall for the second time. They had been delighted after they were first introduced that now they had an Auntie Jarinda and an Uncle Aaron who were so known to all the village children. It seemed to them that their family kept growing. The children begged little additional slices of the coffee cake all the adults had been enjoying.

Aaron went back to Garth's question and said all the workers would either carry lunches along or duck home for meals. "But the day after Thanksgiving, per the village council's contract regarding to some uses of the Stone house, there will be Corps of Engineers electricians in to wire the house. All rooms will have as many ceiling lights as they need and also adequate wall socket. And coincidental with this phones will be installed. At a minimum the Marshal's office will have a private phone in his office and a phone in the kitchen and another at the center of the hallway. Downstairs will have two phones. And also a radio antenna will be installed atop the peak of the roof. Garth's office will have a military electric powered radio with a battery backup. And if Burly Dodge visits and has time and the inclination to help the G.I.s, he will receive pay. One more item and I'm through. Jarinda is more or less our principle and on the phone she and Miss Worthington discussed a possible job as a teacher since the number of students gets bigger every year."

The day before Thanksgiving Jarinda came over in the afternoon carrying a small package addressed to Mr. and Mrs. Stone. "This came to our post office yesterday. There's no home delivery in the village; folks wander over to check their boxes. When you and Garth moved in a box was labeled for you but Aaron forgot to tell you about it." Gloria was delighted that there were two leather bound albums with duplicate sets of wedding pictures Herbie had taken. She left one out for coming folks to see and stored away the second for safe keeping.

A caravan of expected guests from Stillwell arrived in the mid-morning of Thanksgiving. Burly chauffeured Penny, Heidi and Herbie, and Erica in his Buick. They also had along a house-trained young female cocker spaniel called Taffy who loved everybody she met. The O-Connors rode in a borrowed delivery van and had a well-padded and secured load of luggage, crates, and tool boxes. Dr. Williams and Nurse Hillman hitched a ride with Rev. Herman Michaels and his wife Bertha.

Beside the thirteen who came from Stillwell there were twelve more who were seated at the dinner table. The six Tootoosees, the four Stones, and retired Dr. Morgan Velderink and his wife and long term partner RN Dawn

Morningstar whose original family name was an almost unpronounceable Hopi derivative. This Dr. had sold his thriving practice in Los Angeles for the quiet chance of living as part of Ottawa Village which could often need a GP.

Gloria had been mainly responsible for such things as roasting the turkey and dressing and setting up most of the rest of the menu, but at least eight village ladies under the leadership of Jarinda had prepared the bread and rolls and pies etcetera for the feast which began at one o'clock. Rev. Michaels gave thanks after allowing time for any who wished to recite multiplied blessings.

Unexpected blessings were shared by Burly as folks were enjoying dessert.

"I have good news to share. First of all the Mayor has opened up to me a whole big heap of work including helping with the wiring and phones. And what pleases me more is that there is a serious full time job available for Penny to teach in the Village School.

"But for the next thing I first had to see Doc to get some courage pills." Then he chuckled and said, "I'm just kidding about that but I almost needed some. Not too long ago I met a kind wise Christian lady like I'd never met before. And I won't call her a thief, but she stole my heart, and later on she admitted that I had stolen hers, too. Then when Garth and Gloria got married a week ago, I couldn't stop myself from daring Penny to do the same with me. And a miracle happened and she agreed. And the Rev. has already set the date for us Wednesday, December 29th. There, I told you and I'm glad." And he very quickly put an arm around her and kissed her which did not surprise her but did bring applause and words of congratulations.

The whole day had been one of mild temperatures and bright sunshine and after the meal little caucuses formed both inside and out for general gabbing and getting better acquainted. Lunch was planned for about eight which would allow departure by nine and arrival in Stillwell before eleven. After a quick approval by the Stone parents, Herbie presented Taffy to the children as a loving gift from Heidi and him.

Two close friends, Heidi and Dharma, could hardly wait to hear anything Gloria wished to speak about relating to her almost total life change. And the Pastor's wife, who had been a great help was there. The new bride had only good things to say. "Of course I was nervous and a little scared. But he told us the home we were moving into should be considered our castle and our children were like royalty and I was the Queen of the castle. And right away he told Mark that now he really and truly had a Daddy and so did Maggie. In Garth's heart it was a permanently settled matter. And he carried me over the threshold like in a romantic novel. And every day it seems the love we have keeps getting deeper and wider.

"Then later after the kids were in bed he explained to me what his father had told him many times about love and how important hugs and kisses are and I had to teach him about those things because he was scared. And he said we'd have to keep on with those good works and also frequently tell each other we loved each other. And as they say sometimes, the frosting on the cake was when he called me beautiful. But I never thought I was anything special.

"From the first time I met him I think God was enlarging my heart toward him but never romantically. I just liked his morality and faith and great affection for the kids. And as trouble pushed against me he was always trying to help. When he actually proposed to me within me it seemed the voice of God was telling me that this was the path that He had set before me.

"And if you think of Garth as a very solemn and serious, let me tell you of one incident I consider as very funny. When Erica did my hair she told him to be sure to brush my hair after I shampooed and dried it. In the buggy coming here I mentioned it and very seriously he told me the only brushing he would be able to do would be with a curry comb. Then a couple of days later when we had plenty of hot water for baths and hair care he came up behind me by my mirror after I dried my hair and held up a filthy curry comb off the floor in the barn and said to sit very still so he could start. In the mirror I saw what he held and I let out a yell and he said 'gotcha' and burst out laughing and I had to laugh with him.

"One other matter that gives me joy is that in general the women and men in the Village consider me as a younger sister and Mark and Maggie every day are getting acquainted with lots of kids. And all the older folks with silver hair expect to be called grandmother or grandfather and the others are considered aunts and uncles. Can you imagine how safe we all feel living at the edge of such a family?"

The two teen Tootoosee boys were glad to take Burly, Mark, and Taffy for a walk to where the proposed Eagle Camp was to be started. There was a small storage shed on site to hold the equipment needed for a survey team which was due after the weekend. Mark was very glad to get acquainted with the older boys and also to give them time to play a bit with Taffy. And the man liked the idea of having two more nephews.

Jarinda requested Morgan and Dawn to become better acquainted with Penny and to make quick visits to the old school house in the village and also the newer class rooms in the Stone basement. Jarinda also had Dr. Williams and his assistant Ruth tag along. With four medical people taking a look it was quite certain there would be no unhealthy conditions. Penelope Harmonia was very pleased to see an upright piano in one of the rooms and declared she could also offer lessons to students or even develop a choral group as time went by.

Erica was the eldest woman in the house and by midafternoon she was beginning to droop so she sought a bit of quiet in the master bedroom wherein Granny's old rocker was. But the young Tootoosee sisters were leading Maggie and Maureen in a silly giggly hide-and-seek time which required a drastic strategy to restore peace and quiet. All four kids agreed to stretch out on the big bed under a soft quilt if the nice lady would rock next to the bed and tell them stories. It didn't take long before silence began to reign and the old gal also curled up under the quilt and had a nice nap.

The next caucus was almost like a jury for Mayor Aaron, Herbert Wilson, Clancy, and Rev. Herman, were jovial antagonists as Garth was expected to reveal the fears and blunders of his wedding to date. They sat around the large table on which had been the great feast and sipped cups of coffee. The Marshal had such a maelstrom of thoughts he could hardly say anything to get started. The very sympathetic Lutheran Pastor helped him get started.

"Son, you needed help to understand what was happening and that is why we stuck to one of the most difficult things to understand. I believe we all agree that God is love and if His love is left out of any human deeds, they might as well never be done. Take it from there, Garth."

"Well, fellows, when I first got acquainted with Heidi she quickly taught me that liking folks doesn't cut it. All we do for the Lord has to display his love in us for others, even if they are vile. And using God's qualifiers, I had to admit that I loved Gloria, but not in a romantic way. And God confronted me with the fact that it was His plan for us to wed. And let me declare to you all that after trusting the Lord for salvation, I have never done anything more important than that. And let me add that my tangled up tongue in no way wants anyone to think that I can even conceive of evilness in her pure heart. And amazingly she has also declared to me that she has felt her love grow for me hour by hour just as mine has for her. My deepest hope and prayer for anyone who marries is that God will put it all together the way only He can. And that goes for you Herbie and that amazing woman who said yes to you."

Many significant matters were taken care of in the time before Christmas. The electrical work was completed, the telephones were all hooked up, the surveying work was completed for Eagle Camp, and the Marshal also obtained a roomy four wheel drive vehicle for business and family use. Also Gloria quickly qualified for a driver's license. The most fun to the family including Taffy was taking rides to Southport for sneaky Christmas shopping. The three females, if you include the dog, rode up front, the two males in back.

The lad confided to his dad that Jesus had given him another wish when the Cocker Spaniel was given to the children. "But I still have another wish and it's a secret and I hope it's for Christmas but sometimes special treats don't come at Christmas like if a special wish had to be baked, it would take summer time before stuff was ripe, only I won't tell so you can just keep guessing."

But the best thing of all was bringing home a Christmas tree with a rainbow assortment of bulbs and appropriate ornaments and shiny tinsel. It was set up halfway to the kitchen and now that there was electricity it was possible to play a newly purchased portable record player and listen to recorded holiday music. Added to the holiday gift lists for the children were a small multitude of hand-carved horse and game animals from skillful villagers.

Two significant gifts for the children from their parents were an American Flyer electric train with three rail tracks and a doll house kit which was secretly assembled by the Tootoosee boys. And after the holiday it was an easy task to find some of the new aunts and uncles who would gladly tend and amuse the Stone kids so the couple could go over to Stillwell for the small wedding ceremony of Burly and Penny performed in the parlor of the Lutheran manse. They spent two nights in the same hotel where other Stones had stayed. The privacy and quietness was amazing.

As the weather permitted, Jesse and Belle were often saddled up so Garth and Maggie could ride on one horse together and Gloria and Mark on the other. But the children each had to perform simple chores after the rides. And many walks were taken and even some snow forts built which the family had to guard against snow ball fights with marauding children.

Actual construction at the Eagle Camp began with a March thaw and it was certain all would be ready for use by the end of May. But the milder days after the snow pile were gone, brought exciting news to Garth. The words he received from his wife gave him mixed emotions. They were beyond his comprehension and he kept going from an awful fear of the unknown to a never before felt ecstasy.

She had asked him to help her check her weight on the scale in the bathroom and said, "Look how I've gained. Would you still love me if I was fat?" He tried to quip by saying something about loving her for better or worse. And then she grabbed him in a fierce hug and said, "We have to go see Dr. Velderink." "How serious is this? And why are you beginning to laugh?" "Because I never thought a Federal Marshal could look like a scaredy-cat. Darling, now I know what Mark's last wish was and it got started when we went to Burly and Penny's wedding and stayed in the hotel. Don't look so dazed. Lover, I'm pregnant. I believe Jesus is using us to make that Christmas wish come true. We're gonna have a baby and the Dr. can help us learn when he or she is due. But I'm guessing it will be a number of weeks after Heidi and Herbie get hitched."

Garth suddenly exclaimed, "Mark can really be devious. I'm sure he deliberately mentioned baked goods to lure us away from the truth. But I can't blame him because we were sure from the start it might be a treat. But it would be wise later on to suggest he be careful what he tells Jesus he is wishing for."

"Sweetheart, it's better if he brings all his thoughts to the Lord. I'm sure you understand that God has a perfect plan and will always deny any desire that brings conflict to how His love keeps working for us."

There were several places of worship in the Village. The largest of the congregations met in the basement of the Stone house. Its name simply was the Ottawa Chapel. And once the knowledge was disseminated about the Nazarene work and their Good Shepherd Shelter for mothers and children, all the places of worship were willing to help by gathering coins to help finance the goal of never neglecting or abusing children or desperate mothers. Penny and Gloria made an awesome pair in opposing political abuses and unfair laws.

When the Stone infant boy was born his birth date was only a week before his sister Maggie. He was a sturdy child and many thought he would be tall like his father. The parents agreed that George should be his name and perhaps he might someday exhibit the good leadership traits of our first president. He was born in August of 1938.

In July of 1941 the Stone couple again became aware that another baby was on the way. Mark was questioned and denied that he had told any such wishes to Jesus this time, but it sounded like a good thing to him. And he could hardly wait for the day when he as the oldest brother could begin to explain to both little ones about important man things like camping and fishing.

At the end of November of 1941, the trainees were well trained in much of their requirements and deserved a short leave which Marshal Stone was glad to permit. With a week off there would still be plenty of time in the last three weeks of December to complete their training. It also seemed like a great time for Gloria and Garth to take a short vacation in Chicago although a few hours of his time would be needed to meet with higher ups.

Mrs. Stone had never been to any city bigger than Eau Claire, Wisconsin, and to spend a few days in The Windy City was past what her imagination could begin to picture. But she did know that her husband had worked there for several years as a Police Officers and he knew his way around. She almost fretted over how expensive it might be but when her husband showed her the extent of their bank balance which had been the result of years of frugality, she relaxed.

Many small but important details including a good checkup on their vehicle by Burly delayed their departure from home until close enough to noon to make sense that they have lunch before leaving. Thus it was late Tuesday afternoon that they were able to check in for their reserved hotel room. And it was also necessary that Garth verify his Wednesday meetings with his higher ups and also an information session to receive critical bulletins from the FBI. But this still left adequate time to visit the Aquarium and see a stellar show at the Planetarium.

On Thursday they gadded along stopping at any stores that took Gloria's interest along Western Avenue which Garth informed her was probably one of the longest streets in the world. But they were back in plenty of time to go to a Technicolor film which had been awarded an academy awards in 1940. They were late having dinner after the lengthy film, Gone with the Wind, which had dazzled both of them as it had so many audiences.

Friday Garth had to take her to ride on the elevated train. That was exciting to her but she admitted to being scared when the tracks went underground into the subway and then back up at Jackson Park where she had a lightning tour of the Museum of Science and Industry. But on the way back he had them get off down town so she could get into Marshall Fields. That was more to her liking than hiking at high speed in the huge museum.

Saturday would be their last day in town and she didn't mind going first to the Field Museum where the most visited section showed animals behind glass in natural habitat. These were not just small animals but even the huge beasts made up awe-inspiring displays. But the next stop was the Lincoln Park Zoo where nothing was motionless unless it was taking a nap.

They did get brochures and post cards wherever they could knowing that very few folks from Stillwell or Eagle Island had ever seen even a fraction of what they had. And she had for the first time in her life eaten lobster or king crab or even oysters in the shell. She also wished there was a place near their home where such scrumptious hot dogs were sold.

There was only one small nuisance as they travelled home on Sunday. The car radio began getting static so much they couldn't enjoy any music programs, especially the good stuff with lots of banjoes and fiddles. Garth was sure it had to be that one of the tubes was burning out. When they arrived home at about eleven, Garth's office was brightly lit up and very conspicuous on his desk was a message that no matter when they arrived it was urgent that Major Colfax, the Marshal's immediate superior be called. When after about a fifteen minute news summary from the Major, Garth relayed the gist of it to his wife, she began to weep and together they knelt to beg God's help for the news given had been of the Japanese attack on Pearl Harbor. Had their car's radio been working; they'd have known much sooner.

All those on leave had been back the previous afternoon and they all knew what had happened including radio news that the United States was declaring war on Japan, Germany, and Italy. And now Garth had well-rehearsed words to give them as they assembled in the mess hall. "Gentlemen, I need to make it clear to you that most folks including prominent leaders are going to incite you to hatred and anger against our enemies. But I am quite sure that every one of you has at one time or another told me that you are believers in the Lord Jesus Christ.

"This gives believers a dilemma for Jesus tells us to love our enemies. You have been told that God is love and He loves every person and hates no one. It is His desire that every person will pledge allegiance to His Son. So is it not expected that there is no room for hate and anger in Jesus' followers? We are to be like the Savior and love the sinner but hate the sin. Is it not so? And is it not love that seeks for the best for the one who is loved?

"It is good to be patriotic. It is good to be brave. It is good to be vigilant. And it is also good to bring harm or even death to those who attack our land, our laws, our kinfolk, and friends. But the best of these is love."

THE END

About the Author

Over 60 years in volunteer work in various denominations. Have served as teacher, youth leader, choir master, deacon, elder, and recently segeant major in the Salvation Army and numerous other positions.

Printed in the United States
By Bookmasters